ROUTLEDGE LIBRARY EDITIONS:
T. S. ELIOT

Volume 4

T. S. ELIOT'S ROMANTIC DILEMMA

T. S. ELIOT'S ROMANTIC DILEMMA

Tradition's Anti-Traditional Elements

EUGENIA M. GUNNER

LONDON AND NEW YORK

First published in 1985 by Garland Publishing, Inc.

This edition first published in 2016
by Routledge
4 Park Square, Milton Park, Abingdon, Oxon OX14 4RN
605 Third Avenue, New York, NY 10017

Routledge is an imprint of the Taylor & Francis Group, an informa business

© 1985 Eugenia M. Gunner

All rights reserved. No part of this book may be reprinted or reproduced or utilised in any form or by any electronic, mechanical, or other means, now known or hereafter invented, including photocopying and recording, or in any information storage or retrieval system, without permission in writing from the publishers.

Trademark notice: Product or corporate names may be trademarks or registered trademarks, and are used only for identification and explanation without intent to infringe.

British Library Cataloguing in Publication Data
A catalogue record for this book is available from the British Library

ISBN: 978-1-138-18484-8 (Set)
ISBN: 978-1-315-64488-2 (Set) (ebk)
ISBN: 978-1-138-12163-8 (Volume 4) (hbk)
ISBN: 978-1-138-12164-5 (Volume 4) (pbk)
ISBN: 978-1-315-65083-8 (Volume 4) (ebk)

Publisher's Note
The publisher has gone to great lengths to ensure the quality of this reprint but points out that some imperfections in the original copies may be apparent.

Disclaimer
The publisher has made every effort to trace copyright holders and would welcome correspondence from those they have been unable to trace.

EUGENIA M. GUNNER

T. S. ELIOT'S ROMANTIC DILEMMA

Tradition's Anti-Traditional Elements

GARLAND PUBLISHING, INC.
NEW YORK & LONDON
1985

© 1985 by Eugenia M. Gunner
All Rights Reserved

Library of Congress Cataloging in Publication Data

Gunner, Eugenia M., 1954–
 T.S. Eliot's romantic dilemma.

(Garland publications in comparative literature)
Bibliography: p.
1. Eliot, T. S. (Thomas Stearns), 1888–1965—
Knowledge—Literature.   2. Eliot, T. S. (Thomas Stearns),
1888–1965. Waste land.   3. Romanticism.   4. English
poetry—19th century—History and criticism.
  I. Title.   II. Series.
PS3509.L43Z68135   1985   821'.912   84-48372
ISBN 0-8240-6703-7 (alk. paper)

The volumes in this series are printed on
acid-free, 250-year-life paper.

Printed in the United States of America

T.S. Eliot's Romantic Dilemma:

Tradition's Anti-Traditional Elements

Eugenia M. Gunner

University of California

Los Angeles

1984

TABLE OF CONTENTS

Introduction 1

I. Naming the Issue 5

II. Tradition, Order, and Romantic Theory 28

III. The Poet-Critic's Traditional Tie 57

IV. Practical Criticism of Romantic Writers 77

V. "Tradition and the Individual Talent" and "The Waste Land": Critical and Poetic Correspondence 99

VI. Coleridge in "The Waste Land" 119

Chapter Notes 146

Selected Bibliography 156

ACKNOWLEDGEMENTS

J.J. Wilhelm, Graduate Director of the Rutgers Department of Comparative Literature, has given me much help and kindness over the years, this project being one very appreciated instance. My thanks also go to John O. McCormick, who directed the original version of this work. And I'm indebted to my colleagues at the UCLA Writing Programs for their generous support, especially to Richard A. Lanham, whose friendship and encouragement have been invaluable.

INTRODUCTION

Pose the issue of Eliot's relationship to Romanticism and scholarly responses are likely to follow one of two routes, the short road or the long. No-nonsense, direct types dismiss the topic as a non-issue; respondents of the same mind, only more reflective, supply a one-liner: Eliot rejected it. A second group, less benign than the first, and less accepting of Eliot's peripatetic method of treating Romanticism, pursue with deadly intent complex arguments designed to reveal the Romantic nature of Eliot's poetic theory and technique. It is as if these types seek revenge on Eliot for not being a nicer person than he presented himself to be in his essays: the goal of disclosing his latent Romanticism appears to be an attempt at public humiliation, satisfying the resentment of those who love to hate him, for they suppose the label "Romantic" would mortify the victim and render the interrogators cunning righters of literary history. Surely some tertium quid is at hand. Since the existence of the issue can be posited (however insecurely) by the existence of critical works treating it, and since both history and logic, as will be discussed later, troublesomely obstruct the view of Eliot as Romantic, a third avenue of approach which permits and directs conflation of the Romantic/anti-Romantic critical traffic needs to be opened.

That Eliot disapproved of Romanticism is obvious from his critical essays; in them, he often appears to reject it absolutely, confident in both his critical superiority and his ability to understand what "it" is. But later critics may well ask, what is Eliot's actual notion of Romanticism, and why did he devote so much

1

of his critical thought to argument against it, which seems a contradictory if not paradoxical pursuit? His understanding of the term and appreciation of the literature changed greatly from the years of his adolescence to his years of scholarly study; his view was increasingly proscriptive, yet he was unable ever to dismiss Romanticism entirely as a critical issue. The conflict in his critical views on Romanticism and his poetic depiction of Romanticism's literary and cultural effects, as one possible reading of "The Waste Land" suggests, reveal an intellectual and poetic dilemma: how does a critic who believes in tradition and ideal order in literature reject any part of literary history, and yet how can he explain the inclusion of the anti-traditional, the Romantic?

In the first two chapters of this study, the issues of Eliot's definition and rejection will be treated. It is necessary to follow Eliot's first exposure to Romanticism, and his reaction to it, through his formal studies and conscious reassessment, to the period of the first critical essays, in order to define the theory of Romanticism as Eliot came to see it. The analysis of his disapproval is in tandem with his definition, for in his essays his typical pattern is posit and attack, although he does not always avoid direct denouncement. Unfortunately, no formal definition and analysis of Eliot's own exist; to arrive at a sense of them, one must isolate in Eliot's articles and essays all the references and asides related to Romantic poets and, less often, theory, and attempt to arrive at Eliot's working definition through them. This theoretical definition may then be placed in the light of his critical theory of tradition in order to illustrate the conflict in his critical thought. The third and fourth chapters compose the tertium quid: Eliot's critical integration of Romanticism into tradition through the notion of the poet-critic.

The relationship of Eliot's view of Romanticism to "The Waste Land," because that poem may be read on one level as an historical structure disrupted by Romantic aesthetics, is the focus of the final chapters, which provide another context for the content of "The Waste Land," adding to the layers of its meaning Eliot's view of Romanticism's effects in literary history. The result of the entire process will be an elucidation of Eliot's struggle to balance his critical rejection of Romantic theory with his implicit acknowledgement that it forms a part of the ideal order of Western literature, and thus that it is inevitably an organic part of his own poetry, at least according to his theory of the traditional relationships of true works of art. Of all of Eliot's poems, it is "The Waste Land" that depicts the struggle between tradition and Romanticism most clearly. But neither in this poem nor in the essays is Eliot's critical and poetic struggle fully resolved.

CHAPTER ONE: NAMING THE ISSUE

I. Eliot, Romanticism, and the Critics

Evaluation of Eliot's criticism during his lifetime was a less common pursuit among scholars than was interpretation of his poetry, as we may expect and consider fitting: the living critic is usually assumed to retain the potential for elaboration and development, and possibly even repudiation and change. An author must become a static fact of history himself before the body of his critical ideas can begin to be assessed in terms of literary history. During his lifetime, he has authority over interpretation (of his critical, not poetic, works). Once he is beyond explaining or defending himself, the real criticism of his criticism begins.

So it has been with Eliot's critical essays; more particularly, so it has been for the issue of his intellectual and creative relationship to Romanticism as it appears in them. Up to the time of his death, little was written about the relationship, with critics accepting Eliot's own pronouncements that he was anti-Romantic, and that what he was for was a more interesting subject of study than was what he was against. No issue was then in evidence, no contradiction needed to be bridged. The theory of Romanticism was at the time (and perhaps is considered still to be) an unsettled, absorbing issue, its definition still a matter for repeated clarification and continuing debate. The appearance of Frank Kermode's Romantic Image in 1957 created an issue, however; if, as he argued, the nature of poetic language had been fundamentally altered by the ascendancy of organicism over mechanism, a phenomenon historically identified with the Romantic movement, then Romanticism held sway over poets into the present day. To be contemporary, indeed to be post-eighteenth century, was to be Romantic.[1]

Eliot's death in 1965 came only one year after the first significant work appeared which confronted the problem of the proclaimed anti-Romantic and the current theory of Romantic endurance: that work was C.K. Stead's The New Poetic.[2] Since then, critical works dealing with Eliot and Romanticism have been produced at increasingly shorter intervals, and this decade has already seen two studies, Edward Lobb's T.S. Eliot and the Romantic Critical Tradition[3] and Eloise Knapp Hay's T.S. Eliot's Negative Way.[4] They continue the argument developed since the time of Kermode and Stead that at the base of Eliot's anti-Romanticism, equally in literary practice, critical theory, and psychological make-up, is a covert Romanticism.

But confusion enters into discussion of the issue when it is approached from a point of view other than literary history. To question how one accounts for Eliot as an anti-Romantic poet-critic during a Romantic age is a valid study, as is inquiry into the broader issue of how Eliot's theory of literary history and tradition agrees with and departs from other contemporary theories. What seem to me to be unfair, and to do violence to Eliot's ideas, are attempts to reduce the complexity of his poems and essays to a single phenomenon, that of Romanticism disguised and rewritten. Such attempts are anti-historical, and since the issue is very much in the domain of literary history, ahistorical methodologies are suspect. Biographical analysis, reliant as it is on personal details of dubious relation to the works of the poet-critic - for example, the equation of Eliot's supposed elitism with the Romantic notion of the genius, or his choice of residence with Romantic exile - also fails to address the real question and is not useful as a means of evaluating the links between Romanticism and Eliot's work.

In studies of specific poems, several critics have indeed argued that Eliot's early work reveals a Romantic foundation in despair for unreachable ideals, the entrapment of the individual in society, and his consequent need for escape; "Prufrock" is most often held up for such argument, although almost all of Eliot's poems have been excerpted for evidence. While textual analysis of his poems allows one to note similarities to certain Romantic poems in terms of technique or theme, it does not help one to explain their significance within the whole of his work. If one forces out of the poems isolated examples of Romantic forms or feelings and uses them as evidence of Eliot's Romanticism, one distorts the unity of the individual poems and invents a false contradiction between Eliot as poet and Eliot as critic.

Criticism of this nature is objectionable for at least two reasons. While one need not make idols of artists, one may assume that in Eliot's case he knew his work at least as well as we do; even if he did not document his critical awareness, we may respect both his erudition and his unarticulated creative intent. Secondly, a critical work that endeavors to reveal an artist's lack of knowledge is responsible for supplying us with the literary significance of that lack. Only if Eliot's supposed misunderstanding of Romanticism helps us to elucidate our view of his poetry is a study of it worthwhile. Criticism whose main purpose is to prove Eliot "wrong" may be itself mistaken.

All of these errors are exemplified in George Bornstein's Transformations of

Romanticism in Yeats, Eliot, and Stevens.[5] The major difficulty in his argument and others of the same order which renders them questionable in terms of validity and usefulness is the frequent implication or outright assertion that Eliot did not realize he was using Romantic forms or ideas and that he did not understand Romanticism to begin with. Bornstein claims, for example, that Eliot's criticism of Shelley is hysterical and foolish railing, that "Eliot's grasp of romanticism was superficial . . . showing a mixture of misinformation and distortion."[6] Furthermore, according to Bornstein, Eliot unwittingly included and propounded in his poetry and criticism many Romantic themes and techniques.

In his study of Eliot, Bornstein employs what is basically a psychoanalytic approach, which seeks to explain Eliot's anti-Romanticism as a conflict between "the fear and fostering of explosive powers within the psyche often associated with imagination."[7] Bornstein charges that Eliot's work depended on a personal contradiction between repression and expression: Eliot as critic and Eliot as poet functioned in a symbiotic manner, the first fulfilling the role of "adult" and "censor," the next that of "adolescent" and "subverter." "Mature" and "immature" are Eliot's actual terms which he uses to differentiate classic from Romantic art. His terms are metaphoric, not psychoanalytic, and they name differences in literary style. But in Bornstein's formulation, Eliot's views on Romanticism are effectively removed from a literary context, and although we may increase conjecture about the man, we gain little in the way of understanding his work and its place in Western tradition. If one does seek only to investigate the man, Bornstein's approach may be helpful. But Bornstein himself insists on a literary application: we are to understand both poetic technique and critical stance in terms of maladaptive behavior. Further, Bornstein depicts Eliot to have worked from the same premise as Bornstein himself does: " . . . for all self-conscious poets, literary history becomes a quest for poetic identity."[8] The lines demarking man, poet, and critic dissolve in such a statement, and it offers no historical sense of what is ultimately an historical issue, from the time of Kermode's work the basis on which we are forced to confront it.

Eliot's comments on Romanticism in his essays and his use of Romanticism in his poetry find their rightful place in the context of his theory of tradition; one must look to the corpus of his essays if one wishes to clarify the place of Romanticism in his thought. The Romantic content of his poetry perhaps signals some use of Romanticism other than imitation or purgation. To consider Eliot a Romantic poet, which is at bottom what Bornstein claims, seems to me an error in historical terms alone: the use of the conventions of one era in the poetry of another does not necessarily indicate prolongation or revival. The conventions that a poet of recognized value does employ are selected usually to produce a new effect. And the repository of conventions permits a poet to choose and reject among them: a tone of despair or self-mockery, or the projection of a speaker's mental state on the environment, does not adequately represent Romanticism, or Symbolism, or any period recognized in the first place through the complexity of technique and style evident in multiple works of art. A critic who accepts an organic theory of art might expect that a given poem would bear traces of the past without being defined by it. As Wellek and Warren write in their chapter on literary history in Theory of Literature, " . . . the survival of a preceding scheme of norms and the anticipations of a following scheme are inevitable."[9] When fundamental elements of language and style such as diction, syntax, imagery, and theme, for example, betray little evidence of the Romantic stamp, as is true of perhaps all of Eliot's mature poetry, then terming him Romantic because of an alleged "Romantic" frame of mind while he composed it is unjustifiable.

Drawing the lines between organic progression, influence, and imitation presents us with a defining difficulty of criticism, and Eliot's essays often do little to help us along to decisions on general matters and may be even less helpful when we come to the task of assessing his own work. Eliot's theory of tradition becomes all the more important, then, as a key to unlocking his system of allusion in his poems and his judgment of Romanticism in his essays. Bornstein acknowledges the difficulty of recognizing imitation from organic relation: " . . . not even the most avid romanticist would want to reduce modernism to a repetition or simple extension of the past. Yet it is possible to argue that modernism is . . . a development of and from romanticism, indebted to its forbear in important ways and departing from it in others; at its best, modernism is often a creative transformation of romanticism, not fully comprehensible without it."[10] His argument seems compatible with Eliot's own in "Tradition and the Individual Talent," that a work of art exists in relation to the works preceding it, that a process of transformation takes place with all truly original works of art, affecting our perception of the new and the old alike. Still, Bornstein insists that Eliot's practice was surreptitious in its use of the ideas of the Romantic poets and critics: "Eliot made off with as many of Coleridge's ideas as possible, like the notions of suspension of disbelief, balance of opposites, and even clerisy, which he later melted down and recast in his own design."[11] One must accept the idea that Eliot rejected the Romantic poets absolutely to accept his use of their theories as a kind of theft. But I think that most critics will choke a bit in the attempt to swallow Bornstein's argument that Eliot's rejection was absolute, an always-dangerous word to apply to his ideas. Eliot's comments on Romanticism are not so systematic as to allow one to generalize fairly or profitably. And the very fact of his critical acumen might suggest to us the need to look beyond the term "Romantic" if we are searching for his means of denoting the valuable content, that is, the traditional elements, of those poets whom we usually name "the Romantics."

An alternate approach to the topic of Eliot and Romanticism is to accept his criticism of it as a simple reaction against Romanticism in general and against the post-Romantic poets such as Swinburne specifically. Generally, such analyses appeared within Eliot's lifetime, before a perception of the whole of his critical and poetic work was possible. But as the historical perspective increases in clarity, the simplicity of the early views becomes unsatisfactory in explaining Eliot's thought on Romanticism. Eliot disliked and critically disapproved of much of post-Romantic English poetry, but his dislike and disapproval went well beyond personal distaste and particular criticism of particular poets. His essays on late nineteenth- and twentieth-century English poetry contain what one might call "symptomatic" criticisms, for his objections did not arise from a sense of questionable new directions in poetic technique or new aesthetic theory. The poetry of Swinburne and Rossetti was the result or "symptom" of a disease introduced in an earlier era, the late eighteenth and early nineteenth century. Eliot's criticism of his contemporaries exists in the context of his sense of the Romantic tradition, which he believed still prevailed in his day; in the same way, his view of the Romantic tradition makes sense only in the context of the Western tradition, for the majority of his critical thought reflects an historical basis. For this reason Romanticism is an inescapable part of Eliot's work which cannot be dismissed critically because he rejected it intellectually.

II. The First Romantic Phase: Adolescence

The difficulty involved in analyzing Eliot's view of Romanticism results from his dual sense of it: he saw it not only as a period in literary history, but also as a symbol. From the historical basis of Romanticism as a reaction against tradition and a redefinition of the self, Romanticism to Eliot became a term describing a state of mind or spirit that questions order and responsibility. The term beyond its literary reference took on psychological and philosophical connotations for him. In fact, the very malleability of the term represented the flaw in Romantic poetry as Eliot criticized it: it was poetry expropriating religion, philosophy, psychology, and even a rudimentary form of sociology. Eliot cited Coleridge as a man who knew too much, who ruined his poetic gift by expending energy in fields inhospitable to it.[12] The self-obliteration of a Werther is the image of Romanticism that Eliot seemed to retain when he discussed the world view as something separate from the literary school. To him, "Romantic" inevitably implied "adolescent." Thus in his critical essays Eliot mixed the two views, the historical and the symbolic. As biographical critics have argued, the mixture does reflect his personal experience to an extent: he came to Romantic poetry as an uncritical adolescent, and he reacted "Romantically," that is, with the all-embracing enthusiasm of the immature mind. But then came the first of his conversions: he was vividly made aware of the "dangers" of Romantic theory and the intellectual inadequacy of the adolescent frame of mind, largely through the teachings of Irving Babbitt.

By the time Eliot began publishing his own essays, his attitude toward Romanticism had been complicated by conflicting "negatives": Romanticism appealed to the immature; it was assailable on formal grounds; it destroyed tradition; and it represented a spiritual tendency to undermine society and culture. From the beginning, Eliot's literary views on Romanticism were rarely free of the symbolic value he attached to it.

In "The Modern Mind," written in 1933, Eliot emphasized his dissatisfaction with the term "Romanticism," discussing

... the dangers of expressing one's meaning in terms of "Romanticism": it is a term which is constantly changing in different contexts, and which is now limited to what appear to be purely literary and purely local problems, now expanding to cover almost the whole of the life of a time and of nearly the whole world. It has perhaps not been observed that in its more comprehensive significance 'Romanticism' comes to include nearly everything that distinguishes the last two hundred and fifty years or so from their predecessors, and includes so much that it ceases to bring with it any praise or blame.[13]

Certainly awareness of the problematic nature of the term "Romanticism" is not new with Eliot nor is Eliot's view new to our perception of him. But his continuing attack of the problem underlines the presence of Romanticism in his thought. He was not a scholar of the period and, by the time he wrote the above essay, he read Romantic literature mainly as reference material subordinate to some other literary issue. His concern was not restricted to scholarly issues in Romantic literature, however; throughout his essays he confronted Romanticism variously as poetic technique, frame of mind, or philosophy, all of which indicates

Romanticism as an organic symbol in Eliot's critical and poetic works.

Of the critics who have noted the preponderance of the terms "immature" and "adolescent" in connection with Eliot's comments on Romanticism, one of the most concise and helpful is Victor Brombert in his study "T.S. Eliot and the Romantic Heresy."[14] Brombert offers a psychoanalytic interpretation not of Eliot but of Eliot's critical ideas on adolescence and immaturity in literature. As Brombert explains, Eliot often perceived Romanticism as a state of mind common to adolescents still green in literary experience. Eliot's earliest definition of Romanticism seems to have been drawn from such immature reactions. In his introduction to The Use of Poetry and the Use of Criticism, Eliot chronicled his own early Romantic reading matter: Fitzgerald's "Omar Khayyam" led him into a "new world of feeling . . . Thereupon I took the usual adolescent course with Byron, Shelley, Keats, Rossetti, Swinburne."[15] Brombert clarifies that this adolescent identification and delight with Romanticism became Eliot's metaphor for the state of mind necessary to the creation and enjoyment of such literature (unlike Bornstein's conclusion that in this remark "Eliot frankly links his literary passion to the onset of sexuality").[16]

Evidence of the first step in the definition's refinement lies in Eliot's subsequent paring of the list of "adolescent" poets to the second generation Romantics. In later years Eliot made few references to Fitzgerald, and those he did make were only glancingly criticial of Fitzgerald's shallow philosophy; Eliot seemed to have achieved a comfortable perspective on Swinburne as critic and poet in the essays focused on those topics. Rossetti was dismissed without any critical discomfort on Eliot's part. But Byron and Shelley, on the other hand, were sources of unending irritation (Keats, luckily as Eliot may have thought, died before producing his mature work and avoided philosophy, and therefore he did not present the problem of division in Eliot's literary/symbolic system).

For the most part, Eliot drew his basic definition of Romanticism from his adolescent reading of Byron and Shelley specifically. Since the adolescent identified himself with the Romantic poet, the adolescent's feelings were accurate reflectors of the true content of Romantic poetry. This meant that the adolescent mind was capable of comprehending the thought of Byron and Shelley. Logically, their scope of thought was therefore narrow and immature. Eliot seems to have used his personal experience as the basis for this syllogistic argument against the poetry of Byron and Shelley. In an essay on Byron in 1937, Eliot recounted his youthful influence which resulted in his critical difficulty:

> It is difficult to return critically to a poet whose poetry was . . . the first boyhood enthusiasm. To be told anecdotes of one's own childhood by an elderly relative is usually tedious; and a return, after many years, to the poetry of Byron is accompanied by a similar gloom: images come before the mind, and the recollection of some verses in the manner of Don Juan, tinged with that disillusion and cynicism only possible at the age of sixteen, which appeared in a school periodical.[17]

Even with the solidification of his own theory of tradition and impersonal art, Eliot could not finally clarify his view of Romanticism in purely historical terms.

"Byron" as an essay is remarkable in the Eliot opus for its tone. Eliot acknowledged his occasional tendency to the stuffy, but "Byron" is ample reward for any number of hours' dry going. It might be viewed as Eliot's nearest stab at psychobiography, despite his denial of interest in Byron's private life. In the first essay on Milton, for example, Eliot brings in the fact of Milton's blindness, but he uses it to the end of a purely literary discussion of how Milton's poetry creates a musical effect. The biographical data in "Byron," on the other hand, is used for psychological inferences about Byron the public figure, whom Eliot could not divorce from the Romantic poet. He cites lines of Byron's poetry as evidence of his adolescent character and his craftiness as "poseur." One cannot separate the literary criticism in the essay from the sense of the man whose work is under study:

> It is . . . impossible to make out of his diabolism anything coherent or rational. He was able to have it both ways, it seems; and to think of himself both as an individual isolated and superior to others because of his own crimes and as a naturally good and generous nature distorted by the crimes committed against it by others. It is this inconstant creature that turns up as the Giaour, the Corsair, Lara, Manfred, and Cain; only as Don Juan does he get nearer to the truth about himself.[18]

Eliot goes on to connect this characteristic to what he perceives is Byron's reworking of his ancestors' Calvinism; this seems biographical indeed. Perhaps we may explain the apparently biographical content by considering that the tone of the essay intentionally reflects a relaxation of Eliot's critical beliefs, which is itself a means of criticizing the subject matter. By treating Byron the man and the poet as indivisible, Eliot implies the major flaw in Byron's work - the encroachment of the personal on the poetic; in addition, by creating the image of Byron as a Romantic individual in the quotidian world, he implicitly criticizes Romanticism and mocks its artistic value, making it appear a fatuous indulgence of the ego at the cost of denying reality. At the point of Eliot's pen, Byron becomes an unsympathetic Quixote.

In "Byron," the confusion of all elements - man, poet, poems, theory - into one figure suggests that Byron may be a symbol of Eliot's beliefs about Romanticism in some contexts. Eliot's references to him evoke images and ideas beyond the individual poet: just as the common term "Byronism" refers to an attitude, Eliot's use of "Byron" may also be symbolic in certain cases. The naiveté of Byron the individual and his art, as Eliot depicts both, attaches the symbol to adolescent experience. At the end of the essay, Eliot reasserts the critical irrelevance of the poet's private life, but in the final sentence he suggests a personal equation of his view of Byron with Prince Hal's of Falstaff's:

. . . his own vices seem to have twin virtues that closely resemble them. With his charlatanism, he has also an unusual frankness; with his pose, he is also a "poète contumace" in a solemn country; with his humbug and self-deception he has also a reckless raffish honesty; he is at once a vulgar patrician and a dignified toss-pot; with all his bogus diabolism and his vanity of pretending to disreputability, he is genuinely superstitious and disreputable.[19]

The equation, most probably intentional on Eliot's part, makes of Eliot a Prince Hal, fond of his adolescent companion and aware of his value, who must turn away from what were personal pleasures to the objective, mature world in order to fulfill a higher calling.

As a critic, Eliot finds value in Byron as a teller of tales, as a versifier, and as a satirist of a particular period of English society; nevertheless, these qualities do not allow Eliot to admit Byron to the literary canon. In the essay, Eliot's diction seems chosen to reflect his sense of Byron's failure to affect the language of English poetry. To praise a section of Don Juan he uses a low-brow image and mundane vocabulary: "The continual banter and mockery . . . serve as an admirable antacid to the high-falutin which in the earlier romances tends to upset the reader's stomach."[20] This quotation follows the charge that, "Of Byron one can say, as of no other English poet of his eminence, that he added nothing to the language, that he discovered nothing in the sounds, and developed nothing in the meaning, of individual words."[21] Here he speaks of the poet, but the former quotation again mixes the literary figure with the symbolic, suggesting that beyond language and meter the critic cannot achieve an objective view of Byron as a particular Romantic poet: his view always includes Byron as a symbol for the adolescent nature of the movement itself. Thus in his own adolescence Eliot formed the basis for his future views and in his own response as a young reader found his metaphor for his later critical attitude.

In his essay "Shelley and Keats" of 1933, Eliot used similar derogatory vocabulary to criticize Shelley (the true focus of the essay; Keats appears as an afterthought). One can see a major difference in Eliot's view of Shelley compared to his treatment of Byron: Shelley is not a symbolic figure but is treated almost entirely as a poet belonging to the continuum of English poetry. Eliot was able to distinguish Shelley's mature works from the immature and found in the former enough beauty of language to dismiss the latter as irrelevant to the tradition. His laudatory remarks on Shelley usually appeared in essays whose subject was some other poet, and Shelley is used as a fixed point in the tradition.[22] In the essay on Shelley, Eliot discussed the problem of reading a poet whose beliefs are not the reader's. If the quality of the beliefs, the level of thought, is acceptable, then the question of agreement does not arise; he argued:

> When the doctrine, theory, belief, or 'view of life' presented in a poem is one which the mind of the reader can accept as coherent, mature, and founded on the facts of experience, it interposes no obstacle to the reader's enjoyment, whether it be one that he accept or deny, approve or deprecate. When it is one which the reader rejects as childish or feeble, it may, for a reader of well-developed mind, set up an almost complete check.[23]

This formula allowed Eliot to read without distaste those works of Shelley which do not propound a "Romantic" view of life. Eliot "saved" a small portion of Shelley's work from the fate of Byron's, which becomes nearly unreadable through the above test. The judgment on Shelley is harsh, for too much of his writing is from the pen of a "schoolboy" and has a corresponding level of thought:

> The ideas of Shelley seem to me always to be ideas of adolescence . . . an enthusiasm for Shelley seems to me also to be an affair of adolescence . . . I find his ideas repellent . . . and the biographical interest which Shelley has also excited makes it difficult to read the poetry without remembering the man: and the man was humourless, pedantic, self-centred, and sometimes almost a blackguard.[24]

Almost ten years later, in "The Music of Poetry," Eliot reiterated that the taste for Shelley is an adolescent taste, inspired more by the man than the poetry.[25] Yet in Eliot's estimation enough of Shelley's lines succeed as poetic language so that no difficulty similar to that of assessing Byron arises. Shelley does not carry a symbolic value equal to Byron's in Eliot's thought. Certain of his poems are useful to exemplify Romantic flaws, but the whole of his work and his personality do not form the concrete basis of Eliot's idea of Romanticism, as did the figure of Byron and the tone, imagery, and ideas of his poetry.

With Eliot, "adolescent" immersion in the Romantic poets seems to have ended with adolescence. He may in part have tired of some of them (although this was less the case with Byron than with others, and critics who hold that Eliot's early poetry has Romantic elements may argue the contrary: Grover Smith, for example, in T.S. Eliot's Poetry and Plays, claims that through 1915 Eliot imitated Byron in his poetry and that the influence of Byron lasted over twenty years).[26] But an adolescent rejection based on boredom would be compatible with Eliot's view of the immature mind, in which taste is not the result of historical thought: "Maturity of mind: this needs history, and the consciousness of history."[27] The adolescent mind makes no attempt to grasp the lasting worth of a work; if a work no longer reflects the adolescent's feelings, or no longer arouses feeling in him, he rejects it.

A new love may have supplanted the Romantics, and, in a sense, Eliot did come under the sway of forces which overpowered his affections. His studies at Harvard gave him new material to work with in a manner more rigorous and satisfying than emotional reaction had been. His actual study of major literary figures such as Dante and Shakespeare provided him with a sense of history and importance which he had not attached to the Romantic poets. He learned mature, objective appreciation of more "classical" writers (as he was later to define the term) and he heard Irving Babbitt demolish Romanticism against the background of the classical, using the very terms "adolescent" and "immature" that were applicable to Eliot's own experience with the literature. Babbitt's critical view of Romanticism seems very nearly to describe as literary technique the emotional experiences Eliot described as his reaction to Romantic poetry. He found in Babbitt's lectures an apparently objective view parallel to his personal one and seems to have accepted most of Babbitt's major contentions. Babbitt was certainly not the sole influence, but it appears that his views were both congenial and useful to Eliot in developing his theory of literary history, a theory which itself may have grown out of a theory of anti-Romanticism.

III. Reaction and Babbitt

Discussions concerning the influence of Babbitt on Eliot generally focus on the issue of humanism, leaving the issue of Romanticism behind as a basic point of agreement between them, secondary to the center of each man's thought. However, Babbitt's views on Romanticism may have been seminal to Eliot's later literary theories; Babbitt offered Romanticism as a kind of negative definition of Eliot's slowly clarifying beliefs about classicism, tradition, and ideal order. Eliot later objected to Babbitt's antithesis of classic/Romantic as a literary distinction, but the antithesis helped Eliot to define his own critical stance, which later merged with his philosophical outlook.

From Babbitt Eliot received a basis of evaluation, one that he maintained poetically at least through the composition of "The Waste Land" and one that is evident in most of his essays up to his overtly Christian period. By ascribing to Romanticism the qualities of immaturity, regression, egotism, sensationalism, and escapism, and by imposing Rousseau as the symbol of the Romantic world view,

Babbitt gave Eliot a prototype for his theory of literary tradition and the ascendancy of culture. Eliot refocused Babbitt's criticism of Romanticism to emphasize the flawed individual and replaced Rousseau with Byron as a poetic and personal symbol of Romanticism. Although the publication of <u>Rousseau and Romanticism</u> came after Eliot's departure from Harvard, at least one scholar's research, that of John D. Margolis in <u>T.S. Eliot's Intellectual Development</u>, shows that Babbitt was already including material to be seen in <u>Rousseau and Romanticism</u> in his lectures at Harvard during Eliot's attendance there, so that the views expressed in the book were very likely the views impressed on Eliot as a student. Babbitt's extreme statements revealed his more than literary criticism of Romanticism. Concerning Babbitt's view of Rousseau, Margolis writes:

> Both the man and the movement were obsessions with him; in Rousseau he saw the source and in romanticism, the codification, of nearly everything he found diseased in modern culture . . . No less than education, contemporary literature and criticism had, Babbitt thought, been corrupted by the influence of romanticism.[28]

Babbitt's method was the model for Eliot's own treatment of Romanticism; Eliot found in one period of literary history his metaphor for a way of life and thought destructive not only to literary tradition but to its necessary correlative, Western culture.

The ideas and in some cases the imagery in <u>Rousseau and Romanticism</u> are echoed in Eliot's early essays and in "The Waste Land" itself. The meaning of "tradition" to the thought of each man is a large topic for comparison and contrast and one treated in full in other works. But another prominent topic which seems relevant to Eliot's critical and poetic thought is Babbitt's analysis of the anti-historical nature of Romanticism. On the critical side, for example, Eliot concurred with Babbitt's condemnation of the "exaltation of the virtues of the primitive ages" and with his deflation of Wordsworth's revolution in poetic diction to neo-neo-classicism.[29] Both were products of a willful disregard of historical thought or continuity. Margolis quoted one of Eliot's early Extension lectures to demonstrate how similar his and Babbitt's ideas on the ahistorical nature of Romanticism really were:

> Romanticism stands for excess in any direction. It splits up into two directions: escape from the world of fact, and devotion to brute fact. The two great currents of the nineteenth century - vague emotionality and the apotheosis of science (realism) - alike spring from Rousseau.[30]

Poetically, in "The Waste Land," Eliot depicted the cultural cost of the anti-historical mind and used Romanticism as the historical origin of the modern world's spiritual decadence and disorientation. Babbitt's railings against the cult of personality, the enshrinement of the ego, are worked into Eliot's formal theory of impersonal art. Babbitt's definition of "Rousseauism" is similar to Eliot's definition of Romanticism in general in that both identify immaturity as the key quality. Rousseau and Byron are the equivalent symbols in each system of thought. Babbitt referred to both Byron and Shelley to illustrate the intentional cultivation of the personality - Byron as poseur - and the corresponding undeveloped taste of the Romantic poet and his reader: "The person who is as much taken by Shelley at forty as he was at twenty has, one may surmise, failed to grow up."[31] Eliot expands on this view in his essays, but his view may have been suggested initially by Babbitt.

By the time he left Harvard, Eliot had his essential view in place. He had found his negative symbol in Byron, had established the foundation for an attack on Romanticism, and had absorbed Babbitt's imagery for Romantic ideas and their effect on literature and culture. Two of those images were to become part of "The Waste Land." Babbitt isolated in Rousseauism the desire to give free play to the sexual impulse, another adolescent quality, but one which is infrequently part of the notion of Romantic love, especially in English and German literature. Eliot did not consider Romantic love to be sexual and observed of Byron that even his Don Juan is rather passive and innocent. But the metaphor of sexual love appears in "The Waste Land" to represent a failure of the spirit and a loss of passion in the world, losses attributable to Romantic philosophy and psychology. Babbitt also referred to Shackleton's Antarctic expedition in his discussion of "emotional Romanticism." Eliot used this image in "The Waste Land," connecting the Romantic imagination with illusion and suicidal subjectivism.

IV. Bradley's Logical Models

In addition to the criticism of subjectivism in literature which he absorbed from Babbitt, Eliot was also studying philosophical alternatives and objections to subjectivism. His academic work in Sanskrit led to his exposure to Buddhist and Hindu philosophy. His reaction against both literary schools and world views dedicated to a belief in self and feeling as primary determiners of reality may have found further legitimacy in the Buddhist view of the illusionary nature of the world of appearance. Analogous to this doctrine and possibly more influential for Eliot were the philosophical arguments of F.H. Bradley, especially those in Appearance and Reality. Major parallels between Bradley's and Eliot's ideas are apparent in Bradley's theory of the Absolute and Eliot's theory of ideal order;

Bradley's insistence on the relative nature of the self with Eliot's rejection of the "unique" Romantic individual; and Bradley's assertion of the inadequacy of feeling as a key to reality and the illogic of transcendentalism with Eliot's equation of Romantic feeling and immature thought, and his images of the "unreal" in "The Waste Land."

Just as Babbitt's views appear seminal to Eliot's theory of tradition, Bradley's description of the Absolute may have suggested Eliot's later view of an ordered sphere of art which was at the same time not static but capable of organic change; Bradley explained:

> . . . everywhere there must be a whole embracing what is related, or there would be no differences and no relation . . . qualities are all different, and, on the other hand, because belonging to one whole, are all forced to come together. And it is only where they come together distantly by the help of a relation, that they cease to conflict.[32]

If one sees the world of art as a whole, then a doctrine of individualism, the Romantic ego, is erroneous. Applying the doctrine to art constitutes more than error, in Bradley's terms: it is illusion. Erroneous views simply do not match reality. But illusion is error in action; it produces actual conflict in the self: "Where experience, inward or outward, clashes with our views, where there arises thus disorder, confusion and pain, we may speak of illusion."[33] In this quotation from Bradley, we might substitute "Romanticism" for "illusion" to approximate Eliot's outlook on Romantic philosophy. Bradley's Absolute gave the self a relative basis. Its participation in the Absolute could be understood logically if not directly experienced on the individual level. Transcendence is illogical since the Absolute is a kind of closed sphere encompassing all: the self is automatically a part of it, and has no place to "transcend" to: ". . . a finite experience already is partially the universe. Hence there is no question here of stepping over a line from one world to another . . . to speak of transcendence into another world is therefore mistaken."[34]

For one who is already approaching rabid anti-Romanticism, Bradley's ideas may be used as final refutation of the practice of Romantic art. Through Babbitt and Bradley, Eliot seemed to have come to a rejection of Romanticism which had a basis in the authority of classicism and the demonstrability of logic. Separately, each standard - the literary and the philosophic - provided a strong argument against Romanticism. But as Eliot increasingly devoted himself to the creation of poetry, the materials at hand and the question of their use did not allow for the rejection of Romanticism. Romanticism was embedded in the history of poetic language, and any new poetry must exist in relation to it. As a poet, Eliot was approaching a not yet apparent paradox: the very standards authorizing rejection also demanded literary and logical acceptance.

Eliot's intellectual and emotional exposure to Romanticism through the 1920's left him with a predominantly negative view. He had not yet found a means of dealing with Romantic thought as part of literary history other than to condemn it as a departure from the mainstream, as an anomaly. Part of his conflict came from the fact that he had not yet confronted Wordsworth and Coleridge as mature poets and thinkers; he was not yet steeped enough in the poetry itself as a poet and critic himself. As he worked increasingly on his own poetry, and as his studies branched into modern French poetry, he discovered that "The kind of poetry that I needed, to teach me the use of my own voice, did not exist in English at all; it was only to be found in French."[35] This quotation is taken from his essay on Yeats. In this, Yeats represents Eliot's own heritage, not in the direction each ultimately followed, but in the similarity of paths taken to serve the individual vision. Eliot considered both Yeats and himself to be poets in a declining age of Romanticism, with which each had to contend. The problems of imitation and derivation forced them to search elsewhere for freshness and belief. Yeats constructed his own symbology; Eliot reconstructed French Symbolist technique. Baudelaire and the Symbolists had themselves attempted to construct a bridge from Romanticism to a new system of aesthetics; by studying their techniques, Eliot came to possess not only his own voice but to reconsider his view of Romanticism. Where his first assessment of Romanticism left him with a yea/nay choice, his reconsideration of it as an element in Baudelaire's poetry and as an influence on the voice of his models allowed him to be selective - to evaluate in an objective and above all a literary way the ideas of the poetry. His point of reference remained the English Romantic poets; Goethe and Poe held an increasing interest for him, the first as a poet-critic, the next as an aesthetician, but Byron, Shelley, Wordsworth, and Coleridge, in this increasing order of esteem, represented Eliot's measures of the movement overall.

CHAPTER TWO: TRADITION, ORDER, AND ROMANTIC THEORY

I. Baudelaire and Symbolism: Romanticism Reviewed

Eliot's apprenticeship to the Symbolists retraced in his poetic experience what Babbitt and Eliot's own adolescence had engraved in him critically. He was an ardent devotee of Symbolism until he matured enough as a critic to recognize his advancement beyond his masters. By 1919, in "Hamlet," he had attached the epithet "adolescent" to the work of Laforgue.[1] But in Laforgue's poetry Eliot encountered the "poseur" reworked from the Romantic prototype; this and subsequent discoveries of Romanticism's literary legacy provided him with a traditional context for the estimation of Romantic ideas. Eliot's view of Romanticism was to a large extent colored by this backward-looking habit: in the context of Symbolist usage, Romanticism took on new meaning.

Among the Symbolists, Baudelaire's poetry was most useful to Eliot in making clear the distinction between "Romantic detritus" and the "really new" voice. It enabled him to read beyond the sense of individual emotion which blocked his enjoyment of the Romantics, for in Baudelaire he observed the transmutation of individual suffering and belief into objective statements. A major critical precept in "Tradition and the Individual Talent" suggests Eliot's study of Symbolism in the context of its Romantic relationship as its source, or as a theoretical parallel to his view of the Romantic/Symbolist synthesis. As the Symbolist poets used alchemical terms to illustrate their aesthetics, and as Eliot illustrated his theory of the impersonal artist as a chemical process transmuting emotions and feelings into objective art, Romanticism could be taken as the emotional or intellectual material of poetry, reworked by the later poet and transformed into the stuff of tradition. By itself, Romantic poetry was unfinished, raw, subjective; after treatment by poets such as Baudelaire, or Eliot himself, it could be objectified and subordinated to real artistic endeavor and production. This formulation of Romanticism as potential art, as material for the later artist to fit into tradition, made for a crucial change in Eliot's approach to Romantic literature, especially to the criticism, since it allowed him to judge objectively and to refrain from rejecting as a matter of course the presence of the personal and emotional in poetry.

If we place Baudelaire's work in the stream of confessional literature - for when Eliot considers Baudelaire's work, he includes, and ostensibly prefers, his prose works, the Journaux intimes in particular - we find not Rousseau's "je" but a kind of aesthetic Augustine. The complaints and laments of Lord Pierrot, usually taken as Laforgue's influence on "Prufrock," perhaps instructed Eliot in terms of poetic technique, but it was Baudelaire, and his "suffering," which first illuminated for Eliot the possibility of self-examination as poetic material in keeping with his notion of impersonality. In his 1930 essay, "Baudelaire," Eliot wrote:

> He was one of those who have great strength, but strength merely to suffer. He could not escape suffering and could not transcend it, so he attracted pain to himself. But what he could do, with that immense passive strength and sensibilities which no pain could impair, was to study his suffering.[2]

The words in this passage which distinguish between the Romantic and Symbolist method are "escape" and "transcend" on the one hand and "study" on the other. The first two imply subjectivism and thus what Eliot's system discounts as a flawed basis for art; Baudelaire's "study," however, embodies the artist's acceptable and necessary attitude. Such a process put to work on individual thought and emotion results in apprehension of a universal human experience, an intimation of the Absolute, as opposed to the Romantic self's unreal world. Ralph Freedman's entry under "Modern Poetics" in the Princeton Encyclopedia of Poetry and Poetics cites Baudelaire's intention to "capture the infinite within the finite limits of his poem . . . personal experience is translated into an aesthetic experience . . . ."[3] Unlike Rousseau's confessions, begun as memoirs, with their focus on the unique self, Baudelaire's self-study seeks out the universal experience, which Eliot quotes in "The Waste Land," the lies, deceit, hypocrisy that make of isolated selves "semblables" and "freres." Baudelaire treats the Romantic delusion of the innocent and unique self as one more shared sin, and in doing so makes it objective material for artistic use.

Eliot's study of Bradley provided a philosophical basis for these ideas. Applying Bradley's terms to Romanticism, one could claim that the Romantic individual wallowed in the residue of feeling, accepting appearance as reality instead of moving beyond the self to find meaning in relation to a whole. The "unique individual" is an illusion; "self" must be relative if it is to have meaning. And once the self is seen in relation to something else, the claim for its uniqueness becomes logically inconsistent. Lewis Freed, discussing Eliot's use of Bradley, explains Bradley's position, which Eliot seems to have adopted and adapted to literary questions:

> Self-realization ... involves the relation of the private self to what Bradley denominates the ideal self or the universal will. It is by the realization of values represented by such a will, values independent of the self in the sense of being objective and not merely subjective, that the private self finds its meaning and worth. In other words, the private self takes on meaning only by its relation to self-transcendent contexts - moral, intellectual, aesthetic, and religious ... Apart from such a universe, there is self-expression, but no self-realization.[4]

These last terms gave Eliot the means to distinguish essentially expressive poetry from poetry which qualified as mature. Feeling and thought must form a duality; meaning would be lessened if feeling predominated without a purpose beyond subjective indulgence. The presence of thought as an intrinsic part of a poem implies the presence of a system behind it. Eliot explained Baudelaire's system as a study of his suffering. Rejecting the argument that Baudelaire was a "Catholic" poet, Eliot saw in Baudelaire's poetry the synthesis of personal vision and Christian universe. Eliot's Baudelaire is a willing, driven scapegoat, who exposes himself to the pain of vision and reveals to the unillumined mankind's true spiritual state; this same theme of suffering and sacrifice in "The Waste Land" comes partly from Baudelaire's poetic presence in the poem. We know that Eliot studied Baudelaire's technique; from that study, he seems to have learned how poetry transforms personal suffering into universal vision, and how Romantic content in poetry can serve a traditional end.

Symbolist techniques suggested to Eliot one possible solution to the problem of poetry's personal content. The dandyism of Baudelaire and his successors differed from the pose of the Romantic "poseur" in that the latter cultivated ego as opposed to idea. For Eliot, the Romantic "self" was not at bottom a literary idea. In "Byron," Eliot demonstrated his inability to separate his sense of Byron the man and Byron the poet; Eliot read the poetry as glorification of the poet, as poetry whose intent was to create an excess of individuality, to lead back to the man intentionally. Even in reading Romantic criticism Eliot complained of the actor evident behind the lines, of the creative mind which read literature vicariously as a reflection of the self: "Such a mind had Goethe, who made of Hamlet a Werther; and such had Coleridge, who made of Hamlet a Coleridge."[5]

Eliot's repugnance at the Byronic figure was well established, but his criticism of Baudelaire makes it clear that he had also come to appreciate the idea of the Byronic figure. When such a figure had no frame of reference beyond itself, it made for poor art; when it suggested a view of life or was a representation of contrasting thoughts united in a single figure, then it constituted an artistic idea. The successful creation of such an idea depended on the intellectual quality of wit, a quality Eliot did not find characteristic of the Romantic age overall. In "Andrew Marvell," Eliot analyzed wit and magniloquence as aspects of traditional poetry. To him, Marvell's wit represented a Latin heritage in European poetry and was impersonal, thereby becoming a "quality of a civilization."[6] His wit is not wit for its own sake or for the sake of displaying the poet's talent (as Eliot must have viewed Byron's). Eliot termed it a "structural decoration of a serious idea."[7] It is this quality which he located in the dandyism of Baudelaire and Laforgue. Writing on the European background of "The Waste Land," Barbara Everett noted, "Writers like Marivaux, Baudelaire and Maeterlinck taught - among other things - how feeling so intense as to be almost hallucinatory might be rendered through wit, through a cool inconsequentiality."[8] Wit is conscious without being self-conscious, even if the self is its conscious subject.

The figure of Prufrock is Eliot's answer to Childe Harold. Analyzing Prufrock's origin, Grover Smith argued, "Postures of dejection in solitude, of grief for the unattainability of an ideal, bear witness to Eliot's Romantic heritage."[9] But Prufrock's recognition of his own absurdity is not a despairing posture; it is unrevealed to others and does not provide the speaker with a vision of himself, with the stereotypical Romantic pose that at once expressed despair but also defined or clarified the speaker's role. To understand the difference, one can consider the great ironic treatments of Romantic posturing throughout Madame Bovary; Léon's vision of a new life in Paris is the most exaggerated: "Il se meubla, dans sa tête, un appartement. Il y mènerait une vie d'artiste! Il y prendrait des leçons de guitare! Il aurait une robe de chambre, un béret basque, des pantofles de velours bleu!"[10] Eliot's Prufrock is not on either side of the stereotypical figure, the melodramatic Byronic hero or the ironic caricature. Unlike Childe Harold and Léon, Prufrock lies more in the tradition of the witty figure as Eliot traced it and changed it, the inadequate hero of a universal struggle, who sees his own incongruity and improbability but who yet also really sees the human condition. The particular vessel may be inadequate to the content, but is at the same time the adequate symbol for the situation. By making of the figure a symbol instead of alter ego, the poet can escape the confines of individuality and Romantic posturing in poetry.

Eliot counterposed symbol and situation to Romantic rumination. Instead of philosophizing about poetic creation, the poet must find the "formula" for an idea or emotion. His praise of the mythic method in his James Joyce essay focuses on

Joyce's narrative technique, one Eliot equated with the best technique. The literary power of Ulysses came not from the artist constantly calling attention to its unique character; it was not a self-referential work, always announcing and examining its own imaginative form. Its power came from its mythic structure, which created "a continuous parallel between contemporaneity and antiquity."[11] The Symbolist belief in the immediacy of perception, in illumination through symbolic transformation, was closer to Eliot's view of how poetry functioned than was the Romantic process of sensual perception leading to transcendental knowledge. Myth and idealism may be juxtaposed to illustrate the difference: concrete objects in myth have an intrinsic symbolic value instead of functioning as signs alone. From a mythic perspective, water is not a metaphor; it *is* the source of life and its "meaning" resides in its concrete reality. An image like Shelley's skylark or Keats's urn stands for an idea and points beyond itself to an ideal world. To transcend is to leave behind, which was not Eliot's purpose in poetry, as a poet or reader; to recognize and evoke meaning in all its fullness was for him the purpose of poetic effort. Given this argument, Joyce's novel therefore may seem more poetic than some Romantic lyrics, for it makes a whole of individual experience, history, religion, and culture. In the same way, in Symbolism, Mallarmé's swan allows for the fullest meaning because it encompasses the concrete and ideal, just as "les fleurs du mal" represent Baudelaire's system of conjoining good and evil.

For Eliot, Baudelaire's importance lies in his example of the poet as creative thinker, which differs from the poet as aesthetician, stylist, didact, and most of all philosopher. Eliot admired in him the ability to conceive a system of belief which incorporated the individual in a larger sphere of universal meaning - in this case, the Christian religion and the culture of the modern city. That Baudelaire's poetry was marked by Romanticism is true; Eliot saw and criticized the "poète maudit" and an overabundance of Romantic gloom. Poems like "Bénédiction," "L'Albatros," and "Don Juan aux enfers" were unconvincing in their depiction of the poet's agony, Eliot thought, and he predictably termed the figure of the poet in each Byronic. A major aesthetic flaw of the Byronic figure, in addition to the many Eliot had already identified, was its derivative nature in post-Romantic poetry. It had not the "strangeness" advocated by Poe nor the surprise of wit in Marvell. Thus it was not traditional; it did not recall earlier related images to the end of emphasizing its new quality. It was regressive and immature. Yet it did not fail as a poetic idea entirely because the suffering figure was not the suffering individual poet, but a system of suffering which led away from the self to a vision of spiritual life. Eliot separated the Romantic leftovers from Baudelaire's poetic freshness according to its universal symbols:

> . . . many of his poems are insufficiently removed from their romantic origins, from Byronic paternity and Satanic fraternity. The "satanism" of the Black Mass was very much in the air; in exhibiting it Baudelaire is the voice of his time; but I would observe that in Baudelaire, as in no one else, it is redeemed by <u>meaning something else</u>. He uses the same paraphernalia, but cannot limit its symbolism even to all that of which he is conscious . . . Baudelaire is concerned not with demons, black masses, and romantic blasphemy, but with the real problem of good and evil . . . the possibility of damnation is so immense a relief . . . that damnation itself is an immediate form of salvation - of salvation from the ennui of modern life, because it at last gives some significance to living. It is this, I believe, that Baudelaire

is trying to express; and it is this which separates him from the modernist Protestantism of Byron and Shelley.[12]

Such criticism suggests that Eliot sought to separate Romantic imagery from Romantic ideas. He could analyze an image objectively by assessing its freshness and aptness, for these are technical, not ideological, issues.

A critical imperative that Eliot faced consisted of finding a way to avoid contradicting his theory of ideal order in literature. His view of Romanticism barred most Romantic poetry from the ranks of really great art, but by eliding the Romantic element in Baudelaire's poetry as occasional imagery, Eliot was able to clarify the truly significant aspect of Baudelaire's work in terms of thought and belief. This critical division gave Eliot greater facility in dealing with Romanticism because it led him to study individual poets instead of a broad movement. In general, he was able to apply traditional categories to the Romantic poets' work so that his blanket disapproval of their thought did not automatically exclude them from the ideal order. But at the time of Eliot's first critical work, The Sacred Wood, he still faced an implicit contradiction. In the introduction Eliot quoted Arnold's criticism of English Romanticism as premature and not lasting because it:

> . . . proceeded without having its proper data, without sufficient material to work with . . . the English poetry of the first quarter of this century, with plenty of energy, plenty of creative force, did not know enough. This makes Byron so empty of matter, Shelley so incoherent, Wordsworth even, profound as he is, so wanting in completeness and variety.[13]

Eliot approved: "This judgment of the Romantic Generation has not, so far as I know, ever been successfully controverted."[14] Eliot's critical ideas depended on the assumption that there was a common school of Romanticism; a general view would enable him to dismiss the whole movement. He seemed to accept Romantic "thought" as containable, if amorphous, and he proceeded to find it insufficent as artistic material.

Further evidence of Eliot's assumption appears in the essay "Imperfect Critics" in The Sacred Wood. In a subsection entitled "A Romantic Aristocrat," Eliot discussed the weakness of George Wyndham's criticism, which he stated lies in its lack of a single approach or perception; the "Romantic," whether as critic or poet, mixed the levels of experience without locating a basis for itself. For Eliot to make such claims he must have considered Romanticism a general tendency in literature, criticism, and philosophy, without regard to history. There is a reductive quality to the term as Eliot employed it throughout the 1920's. In his vocabulary it is synonymous with subjectivism, again a term used in so broad a sense that it implies solipsism. Given Eliot's philosophical training, his view cannot be attributed to want of scholarship. Perhaps he was attempting to avoid what he accused the Romantics of doing: philosophizing in the wrong arena. He argued that metaphysical problems could not form the original basis of poetry, and by equating Romanticism with a philosophical system, he was undercutting its literary validity and defending his extreme stand. Still, he needed a literary basis for his criticism, yet finding such a basis caused a further, more complex problem: he must first fit Romanticism into his theory of tradition and ideal order so as to have a background against which to evaluate it. Thus the problem: one could not then make a blanket claim that Romanticism did not fit into the tradition. As he had done with Baudelaire's poetry, Eliot attempted to solve the problem by regarding Romantic poetry as a divisible mixture of form and ideas. The forms employed by the poets he included in the Romantic group were not untraditional for the most part, he found. Their ideas, however, often were, and they thus excluded themselves from the higher degrees of classic art.

II. Romantic Flaws: Form

Eliot's view of Romantic form again shows the critical influence of Irving Babbitt. In The Masters of Modern French Criticism, Babbitt had criticized impressionism in literature, which exalted an individual standard of taste and caused the rejection of traditional forms. The rejection was called for, theoretically at least, by figures such as Madame de Staël and Chateaubriand. In their prose works, according to Babbitt, the detectable Romantic element lay in their formal inconsistency. He saw in Chateaubriand "a somewhat baffling interplay of classical, psuedo-classical, and romantic elements."[15] The lack of a whole seemed to him typical of Romantic form and thought, a view that Eliot imbibed and reworked. Babbitt argued that the eighteenth and nineteenth centuries were actually periods of literary conservatism. He cited Goethe's witty observation that "Byron . . . showed no respect for any law human or divine except the law of the three unities."[16] In fact, he claimed, close reading showed more theoretical formulation than actual change in form. Eliot used this alleged discrepancy between form and content to criticize Romantic poetry and its influence. Echoing Babbitt's observation, Eliot wrote in his essay on Baudelaire, ". . . the care for perfection of form, among some of the romantic poets of the nineteenth century, was an effort to support, or to conceal from view, an inner disorder."[17] Most Romantic poetry did not achieve the ideal complement of form and content because its thought was subjective, not classical, yet the form was

38

either derived from the classical or was its antithesis: a fragment. The first error resulted from the Romantic poets' attempts to treat philosophy as poetry and vice versa; the second was the product of immaturity. In "The Function of Criticism" in 1923, Eliot declared his sense of the classical and Romantic work as being "the difference between the complete and the fragmentary, the adult and the immature, the orderly and the chaotic."[18]

Eliot's objection to the Romantic fragment may seem inconsistent with his own poetic form - in "The Waste Land" especially - but his objection seems to rest on the Romantic poetic fragment's philosophical basis. Eliot condemned fragments of poems or thoughts that remained individual; they were incomplete in relationship to traditional literature. In this, Eliot differed with the Romantic idea of organicism, specifically with its basis in Leibniz's monadic entities. In Leibniz's formulation, the monad is a complete unit, a kind of clone of the universe. In his essay, "The Development of Leibniz's Monadism," Eliot wrote that monads "tend to become atomic centers of force, particular existences. Hence a tendency to psychologism, to maintain that ideas always find their home in particular minds, that they have a psychological as well as a logical existence."[19] Organicism in Romantic thought defended fragments as dynamic entities. They were not static wholes but unique combinations of individual elements forever in process. But for Eliot, the monad as the basic unit of reality was a logical impossibility; Bradley was his authority on this issue. Leibniz described the monad as a physical unit, but in order to understand its qualities one must see it in relation to something else: as Bradley argued, there are no qualities without relations. Once a relationship is recognized, the object is no longer unique and whole in itself. Eliot seems to have adopted Bradley's belief in an organic whole instead of a monadic entity. The Romantic ego, unique in the sum of its monads, is logically inadmissible, as Bradley argued:

> You cannot, in any sense, know, or perceive, or experience, a term as in relation, unless you have also the other term to which it is related . . . either you have not got any relation of phenomena to anything at all, or else the other term, your thing the Ego, takes its place among the rest. It becomes another event among psychical events.[20]

Lewis Freed helps to clarify Eliot's view as it reflects Bradley's:

> Reality takes the form of an "individual totality" or a "concrete universal." The form is that of an organic whole. The unity of the whole is a universal, and the concreteness lies in the particular parts. Either aspect taken by itself is an abstraction. For the whole lives only in its parts . . . the parts live only in the whole, in which they find their meaning and value.[21]

The difference in the views of organicism is the unique individual basis of the Romantic idea in contrast to the system that changes, but according to some unchanging principle of order. In "Tradition and the Individual Talent," Eliot described his system of the ideal order of literature in terms that suggest Bradley's concept of the Absolute: the whole exists as a whole in an unchanging way even as its particulars alter, affecting the perception of all the elements but not the completeness of the whole. But Eliot's organicism is solely a literary theory, not a philosophical system. Romantic organicism, on the other hand, is a philosophy of subjectivism; it has aesthetic consequences, certainly, but it is not limited to art. The definite division of self and art propounded by Eliot is impossible in Romantic philosophy, and thus much Romantic art, to Eliot, was total confusion. In his essay on Blake, Eliot wrote:

> What his genius required, and what it sadly lacked, was a framework of accepted and traditional ideas which would have prevented him from indulging in a philosophy of his own, and concentrated his attention upon the problems of the poet. Confusion of thought, emotion, and vision is what we find in such a work as "Also Sprach Zarathustra"; it is eminently not a Latin virtue. The concentration resulting from a framework of mythology and theology and philosophy is one of the reasons Dante is a classic, and Blake only a poet of genius.[22]

Eliot's notion of genius unites the individual to an external order where the genius would be the particular addition to the ideal order, but his genius would not form a whole in itself. The recognition and meaning of a genius resides in his organic relationship to the whole. A thinker like Leibniz, on the other hand, would always be "disquieting and dangerous" in Eliot's eyes, because he "represents no one tradition, no one civilization; he is allied to no social or literary tendency; his thought cannot be summed up or placed."[23]

The literary fragment as a Romantic symbol celebrates organic form, individuality, process, and possibility. Its form resists connection to a tradition; as in "Kubla Khan," its source is often otherworldly, intentionally negating tradition. Eliot centered his objections on the form's negative aspect. "The Waste Land," itself formed of fragments, both structurally and symbolically, functions in one way as a reflection of some English and German Romantic poetry's lack of traditional form, which for Eliot may be taken as symbolic: it represents loss, a loss of belief, of direction, and of the historical sense. If the only relation a poem bears to the past is a complete turning away, then it removes itself from evaluation by objective standards. It also destroys the coherence provided by a common sense of poetry, without which, Eliot claims, no new poet can develop. Eliot sees this pattern in eighteenth- and nineteenth-century English poetry:

> The sentimental age began early in the eighteenth century, and continued. The poets revolted against the ratiocinative, the descriptive; they thought and felt by fits, unbalanced; they reflected. In one or two passages of Shelley's "Triumph of Life," in the second "Hyperion," there are traces of a struggle towards unification of sensibility. But Keats and Shelley died, and Tennyson and Browning ruminated.[24]

Without a unified sensibility in poetry, and more broadly without a vital sense of cultural history, the poet cannot escape the individual and remains in Bradley's "closed circle," which Eliot referred to in "The Waste Land" notes.

The poem suggests that this trend in the Romantic age led to the cultural waste land of the twentieth century. Given Eliot's views on poetic form, we can assume that fragments in Romantic poetry to him are insufficiently poetic because they cannot exist beyond the concrete particular. They present an idea or feeling, but the fragmented form prevents the idea or feeling from being objectified and examined critically. Its "formula" is not provided; its "objective correlative" is imperfectly formed. The effect achieved is not a sense of liberation but of the bizarre and alien. Objecting to the form of "vers libre," Eliot insisted that "freedom is only truly freedom when it appears against the background of an artificial limitation."[25] The fragment disdains tradition and suffers in the same way as "vers libre." To Eliot, both are immature forms because they reflect a chaotic state of mind which is typical of the adolescent and the undisciplined, qualities which he argued characterized Romanticism overall.

III. Romantic Flaws: Sensibility

The lack of a unified sensibility is one symptom of the lack of discipline which Eliot noted in most Romantic writers' thought. Before he himself became a theorist of culture and religion, he deprecated any effort of poets to practice more than poetry and the criticism of it. In Romanticism he objected especially to two tendencies: first, he saw too much philosophy in the poetry, and he also decried poetry's encroachment upon religion. The tendency of poets to theorize outside the confines of poetry led Eliot in several cases to praise the poet as a thinker, but at the cost of downgrading his success as a poet. In one of his earliest essays, "The Possibility of a Poetic Drama," the same criticism Eliot made of Goethe's Hamlet he applied to "Faust":

> Goethe's demon inevitably sends us back to Goethe. He embodies a philosophy. A creation of art should not do that: he should replace the philosophy. Goethe has not . . . sacrificed or consecrated his thought to make the drama; the drama is still a means.[26]

Eliot's comment echoes Santayana's judgment on Faust in Three Philosophical Poets: " . . . whatever philosophy of life is indicated in the play, it is but a moral which adorns the tale, without having been the seed of it."[27] By 1944, in "What is A Classic?," Eliot had acknowledged that an educated person needed an acquaintance with the poetry of Goethe, but he still found Goethe's ideas and language to be not of the first, or universal, order, because his work was limited by his age and culture. In 1955, in "Goethe as the Sage," Eliot seemed finally to have found the way to accept Goethe's value without having to accept him as a great poet. In the essay, Eliot announced his reconciliation to Goethe and admitted his bias against the age which characterized his critical and poetic view for most of his post-adolescent life up to this point:

> In time, I came to understand that my quarrel with Goethe was . . . primarily a quarrel with his age; for I had, over the years, found myself alienated from the major English poets of the nineteenth century . . . .[28]

That this announcement was made to an audience at Hamburg University, which had awarded Eliot the Hanseatic Goethe prize, may or may not affect our belief in its sincerity. Eliot treated Baudelaire in much the same manner, extolling his system of thought and his Christian frame of reference. The essay "Baudelaire" was written "to affirm the importance of Baudelaire's prose works"; Eliot wished to give him recognition as a universal author but with a clear statement that such a title did not emphasize poetic achievement alone: "Baudelaire is in fact a greater man than was imagined, though perhaps not such a perfect poet."[29]

Eliot needed to distinguish between historical import and poetic achievement, since much of that which affects history is not in itself valuable; "historical" need not imply excellence when applied to literary endeavor. "Tradition" in literature is the cohesive part of literary history and may constitute a standard of excellence. It is the impelling force, either by imitation, innovation, or reaction, for the continuance of literary history, and tradition may be affected by it in any degree from the non-existent to the revolutionary. One may think of literary history as a horizontal spiral and tradition as a line in its center pushing it forward. Much exists in history that does not intersect with the line of tradition. In Eliot's system, a work remains an oddity without direct connection to the traditional line. That which connects to the line strengthens it even as it alters its features, for it does not alter its nature and does not detach past features from it. Thus tradition is the continuity in what may be a chaotic mixture of events.

Eliot's view of Romanticism in this system amounts to an accusation that the Romantics consciously obliterated the traditional line, which caused the loss of a directional force in literature and the resulting rise of chaos spreading into the present. The tradition was weakened by outright rejection and by the inclusion and substitution of alien material (philosophy especially) for the impelling force. The standard of judgment was no longer functional; all that remained was the spiral stumbling to an eventual stop, made up of individual works with individual value of an immeasurable kind. One might consider "The Waste Land" at this juncture: it seems an attempt to reunite "strands" of tradition so that poetry of objectively determined value may again be written. Eliot held that one attribute of the great poet is his dedication to continuity: " . . . the great poet is . . . one who not merely restores a tradition which has been in abeyance, but one who in his poetry retwines as many straying strands of tradition as posssible."[30] Eliot saw himself as a restorer of the tradition disrupted by Romanticism. Fragments represented to him the ruins of traditional form; the expansion of the material of poetry to and past the bursting point in the Romantic period came about through a confusion of poetic ideas and philosophy.

Eliot acknowledged that the desire to break away from imitation and sentimentalism characteristic of early Romanticism was necessary and potentially beneficial to the tradition. He praised "vision" on the part of the poet insofar as it meant a new formulation of man in relation to spiritual or cultural experience. In 1927, a review of a critical work on Poe gave Eliot occasion to analyze the benefit of the Romantic spirit. He praised Poe as an artist who had made something of Romanticism, in contrast to the spiritual and artistic weakness of Tennyson and Whitman (whom he called "the American Tennyson"):

> . . . the true inheritors of the spirit of Romanticism expressed by Byron (and spirit here implies spirituality) were Poe and Heine and Baudelaire. That is why these three poets are more modern today than any of their contemporaries: in preserving the spirit of Romanticism they preserve the absolute spirit; they provide the explanation of Romanticism and open the way to something else.[31]

Such poets demonstrated that true poetic vision incorporated insight and objective order. But Romanticism stopped to examine insight; its conclusions pointed in the wrong direction: back to the originating mind instead of outward to a validating universal. It created a mystique of meaning, but the meaning fell apart under Eliot's examination:

> . . . the only cure for Romanticism is to analyze it. What is permanent and good in Romanticism is curiosity . . . a curiosity which recognizes that any life, if accurately and profoundly penetrated, is interesting and always strange. Romanticism is a short cut to the strangeness without the reality, and it leads its disciples only back upon themselves.[32]

Analysis of Romantic thought produces proof of the life instinct, man's fascination with himself and his world. Eliot sought to establish that principle in his poetry, beginning with its earliest illustration in vegetation myths. He saw continuous expression of man's fascinated absorption in the life process throughout literary history. Its continuity was for him the essential and important part. He believed that the Romantics, on the other hand, ignored the ever-emerging pattern in favor of the particulars, another aspect of their ahistorical approach. In Byron, for example, the predilection was evinced in the depiction of private, isolating sin as opposed to the problem of good and evil as Baudelaire encountered it; a more clashing opposition is found in Coleridge's Mariner, who is an unwilling sacrificial victim, unlike Baudelaire the willing seeker and scapegoat. The Mariner finds absolution and salvation without intention or effort, in monstrous disproportion to the effort and motivation of Dante's poetic voice throughout the Commedia. This kind of moral weakness on the poet's part lessened the value of Romantic poetry and made the poets less important:

> The effort to construct a dream-world, which alters English poetry so greatly in the nineteenth century, a dream-world utterly different from the visionary realities of the Vita Nuova or of the poetry of Dante's contemporaries, is a problem of which various explanations may no doubt be found; in any case, the result makes a poet of the nineteenth century, of the same size as Marvell, a more trivial and less serious figure.[33]

By its nature, a "dream-world" is subjective, and subjectivity creates a vacuum where stability of meaning is impossible because meaning itself is sucked out even as it is introduced. Eliot read Romantic poetry not as a recreative act but as a hopeless repetition of the poet's long-gone feeling. For him it had little if any connection to reality and was more in the order of historical document than part of a living tradition. "New" and "fresh" as some Romantic perceptions may have been, the change quickly became imperceptible because innovation needs a context if it is to be recognized: poetry needs to be embedded in a tradition for its freshness to be clarified and its meaning to grow. Without formal relationship to tradition, a new body of poetry can rarely escape sterility:

> The nineteenth century had a good many fresh impressions: but it had no form in which to confine them. Two men, Wordsworth and Browning, hammered out forms for themselves - personal forms, "The Excursion,"

"Sordello," "The Ring and the Book," "Dramatic Monologues"; but no man can invent a form, create a taste for it, and perfect it too.[34]

The poet without a direct tie to tradition cannot justify his poetic form; he tends, like Shelley and Keats, Eliot complained, to try a multitude of forms, and in each effort he is either mistaken or lucky, perhaps not knowing himself which result he has achieved.

Romantic dissatisfaction with traditional forms was in part due to a new sense of purpose in poetry. The poet became an interpreter of idealism and his poetry became a type of political discourse: the mixture of poetry and philosophy was an error in theory and produced imperfect forms in practice (Eliot had in mind German and English poetry, Coleridge's in particular). Eliot regarded philosophy and poetry as separate activites in terms of origin and method; the results of each activity need different forms of expression. Eliot had himself chosen between the two early in his own career, apparently aware of the difficulty of mastering poetic technique and logical discourse concurrently. The forms of art could not be applied to philosophy successfully, nor those of philosophy to art. Philosophy drew on reason in such a way that, if applied to literature, it would produce "devotion to brute fact"; one result of doing so was realism, the "apotheosis of science."[35] The mental activity demanded by philosophy cannot but interfere with creative artistic thought, Eliot believed; it distracted the poet and its result in his work would be to divert the reader's attention from the poem to the extrinsic ideas and the poet himself as a thinker, not a literary artist - the "Goethe as Sage" dilemma. A poet may deal with philosophical ideas as poetic material, as did Dante, or may do without philosophy, as Eliot considered to be the case with Shakespeare. In "Dante," Eliot made a distinction between treating philosophical ideas and developing them in poetry: "The poet can deal with philosophic ideas, not as matter for argument, but as matter for inspection. The original form of a philosophy cannot be poetic. But poetry can be penetrated by a philosophic idea."[36] The issue is one of proper form: a poem has a different system of meaning than that of a philosophic argument; its aesthetic meaning as a whole should prevail over its intellectual content. If, however, a poet writes out of a philosophic basis in subjectivism, then how difficult it becomes to make divisions between thought, feeling, and imagery in his poem, to denominate one group of elements the aesthetic whole and to observe the "philosophic idea" for its maturity and technical integrity apart from one's own belief. Eliot found "Kubla Khan" a poetic failure, for the thought behind it was confused, in addition to being immature and undisciplined, and it thus caused the poem's defective form. Since the thought and form were unacceptable, feeling alone became the poem's strength, yet for Eliot the feeling remained unconnected to either a philosophical system or a literary tradition which could make the poem meaningful for the reader. In "Tradition and the Individual Talent," he argued, ". . . any semi-ethical criterion of 'sublimity' misses the mark."[37]

As was often the case in Romantic poetry, a poem may consist of the poet examining the creative process which produced it. Eliot objected to this kind of poem when it crossed over into a philosophical or pseudo-mystical elaboration. "Kubla Khan" can be read in either of the two ways, both of which become self-referential instead of universal. Neither the poem nor the philosophy is then clear. Subjective poetry always violated Eliot's belief in the need for the poet's "self-sacrifice." The attempt to be more than a poet was misguided and ruinous:

I believe that for a poet to be also a philosopher he would have to be virtually two men . . . Coleridge is the apparent example, but I believe that he was only able to exercise the one activity at the expense of the other. A poet may borrow a philosophy or he may do without one. It is when he philosophizes upon his own poetic insight that he is apt to go wrong.[38]

Eliot rejected the famous final lines of Keat's "Ode on a Grecian Urn" as being poetically, and even grammatically, meaningless, calling them "a serious blemish on a beautiful poem."[39] Philosophical statements, according to Eliot, represent a failure of the imagination and a loss of poetic meaning through the loss of truly poetic language.

Again the main difficulty in discussing Eliot's criticism of Romantic philosophy is the lack of any direct discussion of his own on the subject. He had read some of the German idealist philosophers and English authors influenced by them; he mentioned Hegel, Fichte, and Hartley, adding he had only read "some" of their writing and then had "forgotten it," a rather blatant statement on his part of their unimportant and possibly erroneous views.[40] He rejected any philosophical system in which the self provided the standard of judgment, which is subjectivism very broadly defined. He did not argue against the individual's isolation as the basic unit of reality, but he saw that unit as insufficient foundation for a system of values, for many of the very reasons the Romantics celebrated it. Each individual perceives the world differently and has feelings of differing order, indicators of genius to the Romantic but of delusion to Eliot; the individual exists in relationship to Nature, to many Romantic poets a position of power, to Eliot a demonstration of the unit's insignificance and need for a sense of an objective world; their differing views of Nature also form the basis for their differing attitudes toward divinity. And the individual is born into a social organization, a spur to the Romantic assertion of self, but to Eliot an historical entity giving definition and meaning through its traditional base.

In place of "individual" Eliot advocated at first an ideal of "humanity," a term carrying the connotations of accumulated knowledge and shared experience. He later argued that the most fulfilling experience was that of religion, which allowed for individual worth through the individual's participation in a divine system. Perception of a spiritual world was merely a first step, not a deliverance; Eliot objected to Emerson's sense of religion because it prevented the separation of the individual man and universal soul. In F.O. Matthiessen's words, "Eliot was . . . dissatisfied with the undefined spirituality of Emerson . . . the tenets . . . led logically to an inhuman extreme of individualism . . . ."[41] The sacrifice of the artist's individuality in the work of artistic creation reflected the sacrifice of the individual's circumstances to the universals of religion. Release for Eliot meant the "extinction of personality" through sacrifice, whereas he saw Romantic release to be a radical expression of self at the sacrifice of traditional life. In art and religion he praised individual humility for the greater purpose of affirming general truths. To celebrate individual perception was to rejoice in isolation, which could never be truly fulfilling, evidence of which Eliot saw in the Romantic poets' efforts to communicate the individual truth. It was an impossible task; Eliot cited an example: "It came to me that 'Nature' to Wordsworth and to Goethe meant much the same thing, that it meant something which they had experienced - and which I had not experienced - and that they were both trying to express something that, even for men so exceptionally endowed with the gift of speech, was ultimately ineffable."[42] Their perceptions caused a sense of alienation on the part of the later reader, despite their desire to disclose and instruct. Their belief and method were too personal - they did not partake of or express a universally recognizable truth. The individual could not evoke the ineffable; it became apprehendable only through the whole of a tradition, not the particularity of a single work of art.

Eliot dated the beginning of the modern period from the Romantic age, not because Romanticism signified an advance in language, form, or psychological development, but because it introduced the age of the individual in isolation from tradition. "Modern" to him indicated a state of alienation, chaos, and perversion. It was a time of saturnalia without enjoyment or purgation. No recognition of social order or religious convention was possible. The main feature of the modern mind was its mistaken devotions and inappropriate responses - to the self, others, art, and religion. Eliot cited Rousseau as a contrast to Dante to exemplify the condition of modernity:

> When I say the "modern mind," I mean the minds of those who have read such a document as Rousseau's Confessions. The modern mind can understand the "confession," that is, the literal account of oneself . . . "personalities" succeed one another in interest. It is difficult to conceive of an age . . . when human beings cared somewhat about the salvation of the "soul," but not about each other as "personalities."[43]

The Romantic poet was the prototype for modern man, his poems the models for his attitude. His subjectivism became the common denominator of Romanticism into the twentieth century. Without a unifying belief, modern man - and his literature - could make no progress toward order, which Eliot truly believed was the only path to final salvation. Romanticism was guilty of promulgating a belief in despair, that being human meant being forever unsatisfied, and concurrently of advocating false means of escape. The first influence, or "dark" Romanticism, came in quantities leading to saturation from Byron, with his glorification of individuality through insuperable sin and guilt, the acceptance of isolation, and the notion that despair itself was a way of life reflecting strength and sanctity. Eliot could not bear the intellectual falsity of such a position, for he saw it as a willful delusion carried out at the expense of man's ability to think and grow. Eliot lacked sympathy with the "Romantic agony" because ". . . in much Romantic poetry the sadness is due to the exploitation of the fact that no human relations are adequate to human desires, but also to the disbelief in any further object for human desires than that which, being human, fails to satisfy them."[44] The love of St. Preux for Julie, Werther for Charlotte, Novalis' pursuit of the blue flower, Ahab's of the whale, Coleridge's dejection, all of these devotions and quests were designed from the start to stimulate feelings of exquisite failure, self-indulgent statements of the individual ability to dream beyond the realm of possible attainment. Eliot's rejection of Romantic sadness is reminiscent of Bradley's dismissal of despairing philosophies: "I am so bold as to believe that we have a knowledge of the Absolute, certain and real, though I am sure that our comprehension is miserably incomplete. But I dissent emphatically from the conclusion that because imperfect, it is worthless."[45]

Perhaps with Bradley in mind, Eliot dismissed Romantic despair as having a heretical and hypocritical basis: "dark" Romanticism first denied paths to salvation such as Eliot saw in organized religion, and then, by limiting the route to salvation to an individual effort of feeling, it ensured a tragic stand, a mockery of salvation's true tragedy as Eliot believed in it. The despairing Romantic excluded himself from reality by indulging in a privately created suffering instead of confronting the universal pattern of individual sacrifice in return for collective redemption and regeneration. Recognizing the pattern was painful; in The Cocktail Party, Eliot included a line stating that an honest mind was itself a cause of suffering.[46] But without honesty, with merely subjective beliefs, man loses touch with reality: "Can we love / Something created by our own imagination? / Are we all in fact unloving and unlovable? / Then one is alone, and if one is alone / Then love and beloved are equally unreal / And the dreamer is no more real than his dreams."[47] The inward world is incomplete and mortal; if taken as the basis of reality, it is a dangerous prison of false imagining and self-deception, leading one to identify the universe with oneself, as Eliot accused Nietzsche of doing.[48]

Of the means of false escape which Eliot counted as part of the Romantic deception, transcendentalism stood as the primary example. He disagreed with Rousseauistic estimations of natural man, or the "inner voice," as he discussed it in "The Function of Criticism," on two bases. First, the individual is incomplete; he cannot look within for greater knowledge or deliverance. And next, that kind of knowledge and authority exists only in an external spiritual order for which man had to suffer the loss of self if he desired to share in it. Transcendentalism was a limited and obscuring doctrine; it led neither to salvation nor to a revelation of error. Belief in it "drugged" the mind, just as Coleridge was "drugged" by metaphysics.[49] It was a "paradis artificiel" and a heterodoxy because it was unconnected to the Western tradition. Ethel F. Cornwell, in The Still Point, explained Eliot's objections in terms of transcendentalism's subjective strictures: "Eliot elaborates upon the means of reaching the still point; the ecstatic moment is but one of the means. Coleridge, on the other hand, as a Romantic who will never separate 'deep feeling' from 'deep thinking,' seeks the still point only in

54

terms of what Eliot calls the ecstatic moment."[50] Romanticism taken to the extreme collapses in on itself, like a black hole; there is no means of deliverance from this process of implosion. Like Werther, the Romantic believer follows a path of annihilation and the ensuing exclusion from beatitude.

To be a defender of Romanticism for Eliot was to be a flayer of tradition and thus a cultural suicide. By regarding works of art as separate outgrowths of genius the Romantic cut himself out of the organic whole of art, not only for the moment but also possibly for the future as well. Eliot saw no future in Romanticism because the poets themselves did not acknowledge a tradition and emphasized immediacy over temporal continuity. Eliot tried in his own poetry to nourish tradition and to protect its fate; he warned, "If we cease to believe in the future, the past will cease to be fully _our_ past: it would become the past of a dead civilization."[51] He was emphatic in his belief that a sense of time was crucial for artistic achievement: "We may expect the language to approach maturity at the moment when men have a critical sense of the past, a confidence in the present, and no conscious doubt of the future. In literature, this means that the poet is aware of his predecessors, and that we are aware of the predecessors behind his work . . . ."[52] This is the system of "organic wholes" which Eliot supported and sought to impose as a solution to Romanticism and its heritage. The "predecessors" referred to were not individual artists but "individual works of literary art, and the works of individual artists," the Aeneid in relation to the epic form, and Racine's Phèdre, for example, instead of Byron, or Shelley, or any other "personality."[53]

Eliot's struggle with Romanticism continued throughout his life. He was mainly consistent in his condemnation of it in poetry, but he seemed ever dissatisfied with the intellectual basis of his view. His own theory of literature demanded that he accept his Romantic heritage. The collision of belief in tradition on the one hand and repulsion at his heritage on the other perhaps suggested to Eliot the historical struggle for "The Waste Land" as well as its tone of personal and cultural despair. Still, despite his belief in order, his conflict with Romanticism was enriching for him creatively and critically. He apparently had some personal reaction to it at various points in his life; the personal sympathy and objective proscription were perhaps effective irritants to one who believed in a bond between suffering and creativity. The critic insisted, " Romanticism will not do in literature. The Arts insist that a man shall dispose of all that he has . . . and follow art alone," but at times he admitted that the choice involved discipline of the self: "there may be a good deal to be said for Romanticism in life, there is no place for it in letters."[54] Still, Eliot's crusade against Romanticism's continuance in contemporary literature did not alter the literary history of it. To find a compromise between Romanticism as a symbol and individual works of art in the Romantic age, Eliot turned to Coleridge and Wordsworth, whose work could be approached as part of another kind of tradition, that of the poet-critic.

CHAPTER THREE: THE POET-CRITIC'S TRADITIONAL TIE

In some of his finest and best known essays, Eliot addressed what he termed the function of criticism. In an essay of 1920, "The Perfect Critic," Eliot charted the possible reactions and intellectual directions open to a critic for dealing with his literary impressions. One option for the critic was to "create something else" out of the artistic material before him.[1] Eliot argued against this approach, however, stating that it revealed next to nothing about the work supposedly under study; it had more to do with an unfulfilled creative wish on the part of the alleged critic, or became an indulgence of his personal, individual emotions. The practitioner of this approach engages in "impressionistic criticism," which Eliot equated with "aesthetic criticism," adding both up by implication to "bad criticism." At the start of his discussion, Eliot used the succession of Pater, Swinburne, and Symons as a means of pinning the term to specific authors and works. But beyond these three he did not discuss impressionism in connection to a specific period of literature, such as Victorian prose or Symbolism. Instead Eliot seemed to treat Impressionism as an attitude toward art. His use of the term in such a way extracts it from literary history and assigns it an intellectual value. Eliot's treatment of Byron, discussed in the previous chapter, suggests that Eliot used a similar technique in the later essay: in "Byron," Byron comes to symbolize a world view apart from actual literary history.

This phenomenon in Eliot's criticism seems to be a partial answer to the apparent contradiction of tradition containing anti-traditional literature, since it may provide a logical basis for integration of Romantic writers into the Western tradition, which was Eliot's particular difficulty. If "impressionism" can be used to symbolize a flawed critical approach instead of a term indicating a certain age, then it can be used as a negative definition, a foil for a theory of "true" criticism, which in turn defies historical limitations. Critics who define the standards or at least embody the practices of "true" criticism are the preservers of tradition and become, therefore, themselves traditional. The bridge to an equivalence of traditional critic with traditional poet will be dealt with in a later section of this study, but the logical coherence of Eliot's process of integration may now be suggested. For Eliot, it is a matter of denoting "universal" qualities in the thought of a writer whose creative works betray tradition. By isolating universal qualities in the critical ideas of a writer, Eliot provides a framework compatible with his theory of tradition within which the writer's creative works may be read, the "original" content of which remains as literary history, but the universal elements join with tradition. A study of this process may begin with Eliot's analysis of the "imperfect" critic, the impressionistic one, and move on to his notion of the "perfect" critic, or poet-critic. This idea of the poet-critic leads to Eliot's assertion of universal values, and ultimately to the integration of Romanticism in Western tradition.

A balanced critical view - one comprised of the right proportion of the right qualities - appears to be fundamental to Eliot's conception of true criticism. Lack or abundance of essential qualities would cause imperfection in a critic's work. Specifically, an impressionistic critic might fail in two ways: through a lack of those critical qualities which Eliot defined as the source of greatness in Remy de

Gourmont's critical mind, or through the use of those qualities to the end of artistic creativity, making of the work of art under study a personal and thus reductive statement. In Eliot's estimation, Gourmont best displayed the critical combination of "sensitiveness, erudition, sense of fact and sense of history, and generalizing power" which Eliot held up as critically paradigmatic.[2] A lack of balance in the first category, "sensitiveness," might be evinced in the impressionistic critic as morbidity of feeling, a "des Esseintes" analysis of a work of art. In this case, the critic ignores the need to analyze the the work of art's emotion, by itself, through study of its objective correlatives: " . . . a literary critic should have no emotions except those immediately provoked by a work of art . . . ."[3] A critic who fails to make this demand, that the work justify its emotion, has in fact supplied the emotion himself, in kind and degree of his own choosing. To be overly sensitive as a critic is simply adolescent and hence uninteresting, as Eliot implied.

A second cause and effect of sensitiveness out of control might be a frustrated desire for artistic expression. A critic who proceeds in fact as a quasi-critic/quasi-artist might produce in his criticism of a work a plot or character so changed as to be only vaguely related to the original text. Eliot gave the Hamlets of Coleridge and Goethe as examples. Following Eliot's lead, one might also consider, as an example of criticism overcome by an artistic turn, Ruskin's vision of Turner's "Slave Ship," in which he describes action and color that paint a frightening picture of his own sub-conscious, perhaps, but which is a less than accurate perception of Turner's canvas. A lack of sensitiveness, on the other hand, might best be represented by Nahum Tate's version of King Lear, with its "happy ending," or Johnson's general questioning of Shakespeare's taste. Again, the critic needs the ability to detect in the work of art itself the assumptions and beliefs inherent in its form and content: he must be sensitive to the rules of that particular universe. His sensitiveness is first a quality of intellect. Eliot's method requires that the estimation of a work of art in relation to prevailing taste come after an understanding of the work on its own terms: "The end of the enjoyment of poetry is a pure contemplation from which all the accidents of personal emotion are removed; thus we aim to see the object as it really is . . . ."[4] The "object" in this case is the work of art, which exists first on its own terms without external reference. This "pure contemplation" is a necessary skill of the critic.

A critic's lack of erudition seems explainable only in Eliot's view of the necessary ignorance of youth, cured eventually by the accumulation of study and years. Eliot, however, evidently felt that scholarly shortcomings were more common in the history of criticism than was erudition; a "great merit" of Swinburne, Eliot claimed, was that "he was sufficiently interested in his subject matter and knew quite enough about it; and this is a rare combination in English criticism."[5] Erudition cannot "cure" the desire to create, however, and an erudite critic of the impressionistic sort might feel compelled to "philosophize," in Eliot's derogatory sense of the word, in order to relieve an urge which he knows he cannot fulfill satisfactorily on an artistic level. Coleridge and Emerson exercized this quality too often, as Eliot judged in several instances. The distinction of "Fancy" and "Imagination," one Eliot claimed to find inapprehendable, or the "Oversoul," a notion whose transcendental basis Eliot might likely be assumed to reject, may be seen as the products of impressionism and erudition in criticism, and criticism itself becomes so learned it encompasses philosophy, psychology, and religion. Eliot considered the figure of Coleridge late in life, after he had written his greatest poetry: Coleridge's criticism benefited in part from the time he had devoted to the wide reading of others, but it was also marred by his attempt to synthesize in criticism ideas more proper to the poetic process, which he was no longer able to pursue.

To control the impressionistic impulse to create an individual world view based on the critic's immersion in works of art, Eliot added "sense of fact and sense of history," a single concept, as a necessary attribute of the perfect critic. The concept is equivalent to a sense of tradition in its broadest meaning, as in the "Western tradition." "Fact" and "history" together suggest that a critic must know what happened and also why it was significant: he must be aware of the thing itself and its relation to other things that surround it in time. The same structure seen in Eliot's theory of tradition and ideal order is the structure apparent in the perfect critic's method:

> The true generalization is not something superposed upon an accumulation of perceptions; the perceptions do not, in a really appreciative mind, accumulate as a mass, but form themselves as a structure, and criticism is the statement in language of this structure; it is a development of sensibility. The bad criticism, on the other hand, is that which is nothing but an expression of emotion.[6]

Critical prescriptions emanate from the individual's taste, but, to be valid, criticism should instead originate from an understanding of the particular in relation to the individual. In the same way as the true work of art takes its place in the ideal order, valid criticism connects to history, its own age, and the values universal in the order of Western thought. Unsuccessful criticism is individual, anachronistic, or marginal. Eliot assailed Wordsworth's Preface, for example, as not sufficiently aware of its less-than-new aesthetic; Wordsworth's sense of history was not sufficiently realized in his critical work. That which was indeed "new" was presented as that which was important, a distortion of values, according to Eliot. "Novelty" cannot be a criterion of worth, for it emphasizes the merely individual instead of the sense of the present against the background of the past. To trumpet the "new" is to miss the point of criticism or at least to bypass a major responsibiltiy of it. To miss the "big picture" and to exaggerate a present event as "historical" are equal flaws of lack or egotism.

The power of generalization is an intimate part of the sense of fact and history; it allows one to move from fact or text to an abstract structure and to create reciprocal meaning of fact and history, text and tradition. Without this almost scientific approach (and Eliot does refer to the generalizing power or "free intelligence" of Aristotle as the model of this quality; "free intelligence" was Eliot's term describing the ability to apply one's intellectual faculties to issues in diverse fields), the conclusions of a critic are questionable; his chosen method may allow him to dispense with "data," or certain texts, without a sufficient sense of discrimination. Perhaps personal distaste rules, or the desire for a preconceived structure to be proven workable. Over-generalization of the data or structure characterizes much of English criticism, according to Eliot:

> Our earliest criticism, under the influence of classical studies and of Italian critics, made very large assumptions about the nature and function of literature. Poetry was a decorative art, an art for which sometimes extravagant claims were made, but an art in which the same principles seemed to hold good for every civilisation and every society.[7]

Inflation of a generalization about the nature or use of art permitted Wordsworth and Coleridge "to make claims for poetry which reach their highest point of exaggeration in Shelley's famous phrase, 'poets are the unacknowledged legislators of mankind.'"[8] Eliot repeatedly found fault with critical formulations such as these in that they cause the osmosis of poetry into fields increasingly beyond the literary. Eliot located part of the Romantic heritage in Arnold's "sociological" criticism and in the ultimate antithesis of over-generalization: critical anarchy, or "art for art's sake." Eliot's view of the process appears as an accusation; in his view, that doctrine's adherents were guilty of abdicating their intelligence: "This creed might seem a reversion to the simpler faith of an earlier time, in which the poet was like a dentist, a man with a definite job. But it was really a hopeless admission of irresponsibility."[9] Tradition is then maintained by no one: neither the critic nor the artist has an awareness of the work of art in relation to the general structure of Western literature.

In reading Eliot's various references to critics of Western literature, one senses his search to identify some balancing force in the work of critics which would assure a universal basis for the historical context of the best of them. The tendency to compartmentalize literature and to reduce it to artistic formulae was a species of imbalance inscribed in Western tradition through its classical heritage. The criticism of both Horace and Boileau was hampered by the lack of "free intelligence," as Eliot named the quality necessary to an unbiased elucidation of a work of art. Prescriptive criticism offers an overly narrow view because it is time-locked: it represents contemporaneity instead of tradition. Eliot considered that "a precept, such as Horace, or Boileau, gives us, is merely an unfinished analysis. It appears as a law, a rule, because it does not appear in its general form; it is empirical."[10] Descriptive criticism, on the other hand, clarifies the elements of a work of art and allows the observer to arrive at a correct appreciation, a balanced view. Description is the work of the critic and complements the poet's creativity. In each process, objectivity is essential, as Eliot reiterates throughout his essay.

The "perfect critic," then, is sensitive to the work of art in its primary state, its particularity. He knows many works of art in this intensive way. Through the accumulation of literary experiences and facts, and through an understanding of history, he is able to evolve a sense of the whole: his method is "to analyze and construct."[11] The resulting structure ought not to take on a life of its own in that it should not dictate or attempt a philosophic statement. Criticism is a category; many types of criticism exist within the category, but a writer whose ideas extend beyond the category is no longer writing criticism. The criterion for the category of criticism is that it interprets art:

> I have assumed as axiomatic that a creation, a work of art, is autotelic; and that criticism, by definition, is _about_ something other than itself. Hence you cannot fuse criticism with creation. The critical activity finds its highest, its true fulfillment in a kind of union with creation in the labour of the artist.[12]

Outside of the creative process, criticism serves to interpret the world of art; it is inquiry and extrapolation, in the sense that statisticians use the word "extrapolate": "to estimate the value of a variable outside its tabulated or observed range."[13] The critical process of the artist is greater than that of the critic because the former does not rest at a general statement about art but produces art itself, just as the great critic surpasses the poor one: Remy de Gourmont surpasses Arnold because Arnold's "'disinterested endeavor to know' is only a prerequisite of the critic, and is not criticism, which may be the result of such an endeavor."[14] The perfect critic analyzes and constructs; the poet must do the same at the start, and hence is critic as well as poet, but unlike the critic, he takes the process further, into a new category of creation. The power of generalization is crucial to both, first as a principle of inquiry, and ultimately as a power of fusion and transmutation in art.

Both poetic and analytical writing share similar imperatives, such as impersonality and a sense of tradition. What differs is the intention of each: poetry creates something else out of traditional and individual material; criticism "analyzes and constructs" impressions and perceptions of that material in a systematic way in order to permit the critic to return to a work of art with greater understanding. The concerns of the imaginative and critical minds are at bottom the same, however. Order and tradition, in the system Eliot supported, are equally the business of the poet and the critic. Referring to the ideas of "Tradition and the Individual Talent," Eliot wrote in a late essay, "I was then dealing with the artist, and the sense of tradition which, it seemed to me, the artist should have; but it was generally a problem of order, too."[15] No conflict can arise, therefore, if the poet and critic are one; in fact, the poet-critic will be the most reliable critic since "his criticism will be criticism, and not the satisfaction of a suppressed creative wish."[16] In turn, the development of the critical faculty will support the poet-critic's creative work:

> One must recognize the capital importance of criticism in the work of creation itself. Probably, indeed, the larger part of the labor of an author in composing his work is critical labour; the labor of sifting, combining, constructing, expunging, correcting, testing: this frightful toil is as much

critical as creative. I maintain even that the criticism employed by a trained and skilled writer on his own work is the most vital, the highest kind of criticism.[17]

A poet matures along with his sense of history, which is gained through his critical endeavors; a critic develops through the refinement of his analytic skills, which are exercized in the creative process.

The perfect critic is the poet-critic, then. Perhaps the poet-critic is an ideal figure in Eliot's thought because he insures the propagation of tradition through his activity in one or both spheres. In "To Criticize the Critic," Eliot stipulated that the term "poet-critic" be applied to one known in the first place as a poet.[18] The poet clearly is the authority in creative matters, which subsume critical matters. By being recognized in both fields, and by being especially recognized in poetry, the figure achieves eminence to an influential degree. His influence may not be immediate or contemporary, and he may or may not inspire imitators: his influence shows itself in his power to maintain or impose order within tradition, rather than to invent a style or promote a school of thought. The influence of a poet-critic as Eliot discussed it is not merely literary. "Spiritual" might more nearly designate it, if one could give humanistic connotations to that word, or "neo-platonic," in the sense of an informing spirit. In "Baudelaire," Eliot set out to assess not the poet exclusively but also "to affirm the importance of Baudelaire's prose works," with the added purpose of evaluating the qualities that allowed Eliot to claim, "he was universal."[19] A first criterion for universality is the ability to create, to be original, which may sound contradictory, yet that ability assures vitality and an awareness of tradition's organic principle. Development of the critical faculties ensures a balanced vision and the insight to detect tradition's structure. It serves creativity, but exists beyond mutual service; the criticism of a poet-critic should be "distinguished for its own sake, and not merely for any light it may throw upon its author's verse."[20] The synthesizing power of the poet and the generalizing power of the critic, if united in one mind, give that individual the power to perceive the relativity of parts in terms of the whole; his mind is comprehensive and allows him to work within history and above it, in universal terms.

"Generalization" seems to be synonymous with "universality" in Eliot's vocabulary. In "Goethe as the Sage," Eliot analyzed the qualities of the European mind as opposed to the literary representative of a specific language. The universal mind transcends national differences and, what is more, it transcends the historical life: its qualities make it universal at the same time as its application gives cohesion to tradition. The influence of such a figure "is not a matter of historical record only; he will continue to be of value to every Age, and every Age will understand him differently and be compelled to assess his work afresh."[21] Eliot classed Dante, Shakespeare, and Goethe together as universal minds. They are the poetic representatives of Eliot's model, but he does not ally the great qualities of mind exclusively to the creation of poetry: "They would not be great Europeans unless they were great poets, but their greatness as Europeans is more complex, more comprehensive, than their superiority over other poets of their own language."[22] The universality of these figures resides in their poetry and thought; they display a kind of creative power of generalization.

Just as the great mind transcends history, the perfect critic is unhampered by limitations of his age. He is of his age as well as above it. In "The Perfect

Critic," Eliot noted the lack of "free intelligence" in Dryden and the seventeenth-century critics. He criticizes them for "a tendency to legislate."[23] At first, such criticism seems untypical of Eliot and even contradictory, for the effort of legislation expresses one aspect of the neo-classical age, defining it in history and tradition. But as Eliot envisions the perfect critic, he is of an ahistorical nature. Like the great European mind, the critical mind is universal. It appears to be the same quality in each and produces the same effect in all of its manifestations. That Eliot when he discussed the quality of universality was not limiting it to the poet seems evident: " . . . I suspect that when we call any Man of Letters a Great European, we are exceeding the limits of purely literary judgment - we are making an historical, a social and an ethical valuation as well."[24] The qualities remain the same and can be detected in any part of a writer's work. The whole perception will be unified, another term Eliot used to describe the nature of the Great European. Every endeavor, in whatever field, will fit into a coherent point of view; in Eliot's words, "The test of unity is this: does every part of a man's work help us to understand the rest?"[25] Dante ranks among the greatest minds due to the organic relationship of his "political, theological, and moral aims."[26] Shakespeare's works, Eliot claimed, could be understood only with the knowledge of the early plays in relation to the late, as well as knowledge of the late to understand the early. With Goethe, this profession of belief in the unity of thought has its most radical application; Eliot admitted that at first he questioned the value of Goethe's scientific works, but later asserted that unity of thought in the greatest minds does exist in their different kinds of works: " . . . it is not reasonable to dismiss as utter nonsense in the field of scientific inquiry, what we accept as inspired wisdom in poetry."[27]

Many manifestations of the concept of the particular and the universal forming a whole appear throughout Eliot's essays and poems, such as Bradley's theories, the allusions in "The Waste Land," and time in "Four Quartets." In his criticism the parallel appears as history and universality. The best critic and the greatest mind do not "legislate," attempt to limit, or fix our sense of literary value. The function of criticism (and "criticism" comes to refer to a total view, as Eliot envisioned it: "Literary criticism should be completed by criticism from a definite ethical and theological standpoint") is to liberate us from temporal ties, including national identity, so that we can evaluate what is best in our literature according to the universal values of tradition.[28] Eliot attempted to redirect criticism away from irresponsibility and Arnold's sociology. In T.S. Eliot: Aesthetics and History, Lewis Freed noted the ahistorical nature of Eliot's criticism: " Eliot's readaptation of criticism to a concept of order in poetry according to a spiritual valuation supercedes, for him, the Aristotelian view of poetry, the neo-classic, the Romantic, and the Victorian."[29] Eliot's criticism deals with order and disorder, which are not historical terms. Freed also noted that what Eliot found valuable in Wordsworth's Preface was his reference to universal values; Eliot's disapproval of Wordsworth's self-conscious historical challenge has already been noted.

Valuable critical ideas are the product of a certain kind of intellect made up of the right balance of the ideal qualities. The best critical ideas belong to no one period of literary history but are useful in perceiving tradition as a universal entity; they are pure. When Eliot praised Coleridge as a critic, he carefully removed him from an historical context. The following quotation demonstrates Eliot's direct insistence on valuing the critic's mind over his historical background:

"I am not sure that Coleridge learned so much from German philosophers, or earlier from Hartley, as he thought he did; what is best in his criticism seems to come from his own delicacy and subtlety of insight as he reflected upon his own experience of writing poetry."[30] The poet-critic is of the highest value; his frame of reference is not only historical, but universal, in terms of having great mental capacity for perception and generalization, and thus his insights are about traditional values and relate to works beyond his own age. The critics who can achieve such insights can claim universality; their thought places them in the mainstream of tradition. Considered as poets, Coleridge and Wordsworth are outside of tradition, for they are associated with a movement that was destructive to tradition. But they are poet-critics, and they bear consideration as universal minds, which are representative, which maintain order in tradition. In "Wordsworth and Coleridge," Eliot followed this logical pattern of excising thought from history to identify its value in traditional terms:

> Of the two poets as critics, it was Wordsworth who knew better what he was about: his critical insight, in this one Preface and the Supplement, is enough to give him the highest place . . . there is, in his poetry and in his Preface, a profound spiritual revival, an inspiration communicated rather to Pusey and Newman, to Ruskin, and to the great humanitarians, than to the accredited poets of the next age.[31]

Eliot tied Wordsworth and Coleridge to a critical tradition to account for their importance; they were not judged exclusively as Romantic poets, for such judgment must have been negative in the context of Eliot's theory of ideal order. The value of their poetry can be seen only in the context of their critical ideas, which themselves belong to the structure of tradition through their unifying and universal elements.

The poet-critic, so central and eminent a figure in Eliot's thought, comprises more than the sum of two activities; by being creative and critical, he achieves what an earlier age might consider transcendent knowledge:

> The high functions of the intellect are so allied, that some imaginative power usually appears in all eminent minds, even in arithmeticians of the first class, but especially in meditative men of an intuitive habit of thought. This class serve us, so that they have the perception of identity and the perception of reaction. The eyes of Plato, Shakespeare, Swedenborg, Goethe, never shut on either of these laws. The perception of these laws is a kind of meter of the mind.[32]

Thus Emerson defined the "representative man," whose informing spirit is akin to that of the poet-critic. What one might refer to as the history of each figure differs, certainly, but the notion of universality evident in the formulations of both Emerson and Eliot suggests continuity despite history.

If one rereads Emerson's "The Uses of Great Men" with this aspect of Eliot's thought in mind, the parallels are multiple, and justifiable. The common charge exemplified in Victor Brombert's statement, "The entire notion of tradition as expounded by Eliot is flagrantly arbitrary: why leave Romanticism out?," may be countered with the suggestion that careful analysis of the great Romantic works of criticism and theory in light of Eliot's theory of universal values shows there to be no logical inconsistency in his notion of tradition.[33] Eliot "leaves Romanticism out" just as he leaves literary history out of his essays on Seneca, Shakespeare, Milton, and other poets. As a critic he measured the literary merit of each artist according to the material of his art; in the poet's case, language, meter, imagery, and idea are examined strictly within the confines of poetry. The artist as a whole - in relation to tradition as well as to his art - is considered as a deciding factor of greatness: "Shakespeare's principal merit may be conveyed, in saying that he, of all men, best understands the English language, and can say what he will. Yet . . . Shakespeare's name suggests other and purely intellectual benefits."[34] The poetry on its own terms, the poet, and his symbolic relevance in the larger sphere of human concerns: the ideas in the quotation from Emerson are ideas Eliot reiterated at a later time for their universal value. One can elide the specifically Romantic phrasing or emphasis to see the traditional content clearly. Eliot did so in this comment on Wordsworth: "When you find Wordsworth as the seer and prophet whose function it is to instruct and edify through pleasure, as if this were something he had found out for himself, you may begin to think that there is something in it . . . ."[35] The disinterested critic will make no mistake; he will identify the Horatian element, and move from there to an analysis of its latest emanation. The best critic will be objective and will seek to identify the structure inherent in art: " the great man is greater, when he can abolish himself, and all heroes, by letting in this element of reason, irrespective of persons; this subtilizer, and irresistible upward force, into our thought, destroying individualism," as Emerson explained his notion of greatnes.[36] There is nothing metaphysical in Eliot's; Emerson's Romantic content can be identified and considered on its own terms (and be subject to the main objections of individuality and invasion of philosophy); in short, the metaphysics can be studied separately while the essential traditional elements of objectivity, analytic thought, and perception of the whole affirm the value of the work beyond history.

Eliot's criteria of abundance and amplitude in the assessment of a classic are examples of universal values, meaning they can be found elsewhere in tradition. These criteria were also suggested by Emerson, the first in his essays on Montaigne, whom he called "a man with such abundance of thoughts," the second in the opening of his essay on Shakespeare: "Great men are more distinguished by range and extent, than by originality."[37] His very sense of originality suggests Eliot's later comments on that quality; both emphasize that the merely new is not the truly original, for simple unlikeness to others is more cacaphony than art. The great writer is primarily a synthesizer and can perceive order or create it. Emerson called him an "organic agent," a term which aptly describes Eliot's idea of the poet's service to tradition. In "History," Emerson called the poet a "universal man."[38] Beyond these specific echoes, more general beliefs appear as common elements in the thought of the two American writers. Emerson's emphasis on the value of intelligence makes his thought less alien to Eliot's than were some forms of European Romanticism. Emerson's mistrust of the unrestrained ego, seen in his disagreement with Carlyle's version of the "great man" theory of history, further eases the way to a possible community of thought. Finally, Emerson's desire to reveal unity among mankind, historically a Romantic impulse, in essence shares with Eliot a common value of the permanent above the transitory, the whole above the part, and a belief in man's ability to perceive or, for Eliot, conceive of, an absolute. Eliot's expression of these ideas remained within the confines of literary studies, and he did not share Emerson's belief in transcendentalism, among other extra-literary beliefs. He did not claim affinity with Emerson, but such explicit reference would be unnecessary, for Eliot was devoted to the particular value, not the historical expression of it. He was not the heir of Emerson per se, but, like his predecessor, aimed at preserving Western tradition generally.

Eliot named proper interpretation and the correction of taste as the ends of critical activity; to achieve these ends, the critic must command a wide periphery, one wider than a critic who aims to generalize about his age or any single age alone commands. Eliot's thought conforms with Emerson's on the issue of the universality of great minds. A writer like Charles Whibley is not a critic, Eliot wrote in "Imperfect Critics," because the value of his works is restricted to giving the "local flavour" of an age.[39] Eliot did note that such writers are useful in that they keep a taste for some period alive, or may revive it, or help to create it. Without the balancing force of generalizing thought, however, no criticism is achieved. The greatest poet-critics, the universal minds, complete the effort of lesser writers and prevent the breakdown of a tradition beyond the local level. Eliot treated Goethe as a major representation of one who fills this need; Emerson did so earlier and explained the function in this way:

> The great, or such as hold of nature, and transcend fashions, by their fidelity to universal ideas, are saviors from these federal errors, and defend us from our contemporaries. They are the exceptions which we want, where all grows alike. A foreign greatness is the antidote for cabalism.[40]

That there can be uniformity of thought between Eliot and major representatives of Romanticism, and that, in consequence, Eliot's theory of tradition is not arbitrary or logically flawed on this point, depends on one's acceptance of this intellectual construct of the poet-critic whose real value is not necessarily in literary history. Eliot seems to engage the conflict in these terms, and perhaps we must be satisfied with the logic within his system first; evaluating that system itself is not the focus of this study. In Eliot's thought, however, the value of criticism appears to lie in its usefulness for maintaining our sense of tradition, and while criticism itself is not art, it is about art, and this secondary connection to the material of tradition makes its authors traditional. Perhaps it is by virtue of the fact that the greatest criticism applies to the best in art of any age that Eliot seems to feel justified in fastening the true value of some poet-critics to their critical work instead of, and in some cases despite, their poetic material. Eliot derided much of Coleridge's poetry, and claimed that only "Dejection: an Ode" was near to greatness, but Coleridge's critical faculties, which were exercized in poetic work and later in direct criticism, achieved greatness in Eliot's estimation. On that basis alone Coleridge has "eternal value" because he meets the criteria of universality: "No literary criticism can for a future generation excite more than curiosity, unless it continues to be of use in itself to future generations, to have intrinsic value outside of its historical context."[41] If the critical work of a Romantic poet is useful for restoring or maintaining tradition, then that poet represents no logical conflict in Eliot's system. Criticism is an equal of poetry in determining general artistic value. The best praise Eliot offers in the case of Arnold is his reformulation of Arnold's perception of the use of criticism in relation to Romanticism:

> After the prophetic frenzies of the end of the eighteenth and the beginning of the nineteenth century, Arnold seems to come to us saying: "This poetry is very fine, it is opulent and careless, it is sometimes profound, it is highly original; but you will never establish and maintain a tradition if you go on in this haphazard way."[42]

The critic steps in to reimpose order in art; to do so, that critic must have universal vision and will be judged by later critics to be a representative mind, and his reputation - his influence - will be part of the whole of tradition, not simply of his age.

CHAPTER FOUR: PRACTICAL CRITICISM OF ROMANTIC WRITERS

Eliot's structuring of tradition as a whole instead of a simple sequence seems designed to account for apparent aberrations in the thought and work of some very great artists. Romanticism may have been the greatest challenge to the system, since it led Eliot to account for its importance largely through its criticism, not its poetry. At the same time, Eliot seemed concerned with hurrying the demise of any leftover Romantic spirit, in English poetry especially, fulfilling Emerson's prophesy that the "reputations of the nineteenth century will one day be quoted, to prove its barbarism."[1] The early years of his career, approximately through the publication of "The Waste Land," show evidence of Eliot devoting most of his intellectual energy when he dealt with the challenge of Romanticism to the derogation of its poetry and theory. The past and current image of Eliot as the arch anti-Romantic perhaps derives from this period of concentrated criticism of that literary age.

The Use of Poetry, published in 1933, contains the essays which most strongly suggest Eliot's intention to reconcile the best of Romanticism - its poet-critics - with tradition by focusing attention on the universal values of Wordsworth and Coleridge in particular, and later Goethe, thereby separating the valid critical contribution from the poetic affront to tradition. It seems the poet can exercize a destructive influence, but the really good poet-critic will not, by virtue of the universal qualities of his criticism as it is applied to his own works or the works of others. The greatness of his critical mind will palliate the effect of untraditional elements in his poetry, since full understanding of the critical ideas, Eliot stated, comes only in relation to that critic's poetry. It is as if Eliot wished Coleridge, for example, as a critic to guide the reader through the lines of his poetry, since the emphasis then would not be on subjective experience, as reading the poem without the critical guide would be, but instead would provide an objective analysis of the language and technique of the poem first, and then a comparison of it to other poems in tradition, a process which dispenses with the dangers of subjectivism altogether. If Eliot did in fact use terms outside their historical context to name instead symbolic or universal qualities, and if "traditional" partakes of more than literary history, then there is no logical inconsistency in Eliot's rejection of Romanticism and acceptance of certain "Romantic" critics. Eliot could endorse specific points in Romantic poetic theory without being guilty of historical mutilation. He could annex Coleridge's theory of imagination, omitting his notion of fancy and his psychological theory. Wordsworth could be ridiculed for his belief in the naturalness of his poetic language as well as championed for his emphasis on natural poetic diction. In each case, Coleridge, Wordsworth, and Goethe are berated historically but assigned permanent value within tradition.

Aside from "Wordsworth and Coleridge," Eliot wrote no direct criticism of Wordsworth's poetry and poetic theories. He does refer to Wordsworth in other essays, particularly when he discusses poetic diction (as in "The Music of Poetry" and "Johnson as Critic and Poet"). In the context of Wordsworth as critic, and especially considering his statement on the connection of poetic language to everyday speech, Eliot's critical comments clarify the single aspect of

Wordsworth's work that he considered to be valuable in tradition. He did not analyze any of Wordsworth's poems in terms of poetic diction, probably because he judged that not enough of the critic's insight was apparent in it, for "Wordsworth by no means worried himself to excess in observing his own principles."[2] Not all of his poetic principles were of equal merit in any case, as Eliot judged; he rejected, without reservation, the idea of recollection in tranquility as mere reportage of Wordsworth's procedure, a limited and incidental piece of information. Eliot's comments on Wordsworth so often emphasized the importance of his major critical contribution that the figure of the poet and the rest of his work seem to recede into disinterest, an impression that again indicates Eliot's desire to deal in ahistorical concepts of traditional concern. The use to which Wordsworth put his critical insight in his poems - the "technique of feeling," as Eliot named it - demonstrated some limitation of Wordsworth's understanding, which Eliot seemed to suggest by questioning how clearly Wordsworth saw the implications of his criticism for his poetry:

> If Wordsworth thought that he was simply occupied with reform of language, he was deceived; he was occupied with revolution of language; and his own language was as capable of artificiality, and no more capable of naturalness, than that of Pope - as Byron felt, and as Coleridge candidly pointed out.[3]

Eliot noted the same limitation in "Johnson as Critic and Poet":

> Nor does Wordsworth himself evince any more consciousness of the constancy with which language must change, than does Johnson: what he thought he had established was a return to a diction of popular simplicity and rural purity. In his perception that the language of literature must not

lose its connection with the language of speech, Wordsworth was right; but his standard of the right poetic diction was no more relative than Johnson's.[4]

Such comments undermine Wordsworth's authority as a poet, which Eliot seemed to feel sufficiently convinced was a necessity, if English literature was to be guided back to its traditional framework, for the influence of Wordsworth's poetry in itself, on later poetry and criticism both, caused "decadence," or so Eliot claimed in an early review.

Eliot conceded that Wordsworth's experimentation with language and form in his poetry was necessary to test the feasibility of the principle of natural poetic diction. At some point Wordsworth inevitably produced a pedestrian effect in his poetry as he pursued the experiment. But for Eliot, each critical assertion of the principle is revolutionary, regardless of the results in the critic's poetry, because it represents an ideal that may never be attained on the poetic level. Language always changes: "The followers of a revolution develop the new poetic idiom in one direction or another; meanwhile the spoken language goes on changing, and the poetic idiom goes out of date."[5] It is a critical imperative to keep the impulse alive, if tradition is to thrive. Wordsworth's preface ties him to tradition in this way, and Eliot recognized him as a major figure in the Western tradition on that basis almost exclusively. Eliot himself reasserted the same universal value, and stated it more strongly and directly than did Wordsworth:

> There is one law of nature more powerful than . . . varying currents, or influences from abroad or from the past: the law that poetry must not stray too far from the ordinary everyday language which we use and hear . . . poetry cannot afford to lose its contact with the changing language of

common intercourse.[6]

Eliot's statement emphasized the universal value of natural language in poetry and the importance of observing the rule so that poetry does not become alien to our culture: he was concerned with poetry's continuing existence. Eliot's belief that "poetry must not stray too far" from common language differs from Wordsworth's announced purpose to "adopt the very language of men," in that Eliot intended his theory to be purely literary, while he saw in Wordsworth's a social intention as well: " . . . it is Wordsworth's social interest that inspires his own novelty of form in verse, and backs up his explicit remarks upon poetic diction; and it is really this social interest which . . . the fuss was all about."[7] Natural language should not be associated with Romanticism, Eliot seemed to imply; Wordsworth was reasserting a principle evident in the English poetic tradition at least since Dryden. The particular historical context of Wordsworth showed that his perception of the traditional value of common language was not completely literary and was tinged with some typical Romantic flaws. Wordsworth's reputation should rest on his recognition of the universal value and be tempered by the observation that the concept itself was not given existence and value by him: poetry over personality. Great poet-critics for Eliot embody the highest point of synthetic thought; they represent traditional ideas, not idols, a belief Eliot held in common with Emerson: "The power which great men communicate is not theirs. When we are exalted by ideas, we do not owe this to Plato, but to the idea, to which Plato was also a debtor."[8]

Wordsworth is an eminent figure to Eliot because of his single critical assertion of natural poetic diction, for it displays the continuity of the English poetic tradition. He admired Wordsworth as a poet-critic, if not directly as a poet. Eliot stated several times that Wordsworth wrote the Preface to the <u>Lyrical Ballads</u> to justify his poetry; a kind of worth repairs to the poetry from the great critical insight that it helped to produce. Insights such as Wordsworth's appear to be new at each proclamation because they refine the principle, or color it with the "local flavour," or because the principle has been obscured through inferior poetic and critical practice. While Wordsworth believed (or Eliot believed he did) that his theory of poetic diction was original, Eliot issued his own reaffirmation of it with insistence on its traditional nature:

> I think that Ezra Pound and I believed that we were affirming forgotten standards, rather than setting up new idols. Wordsworth, when he said that his purpose was "to imitate, and as far as possible, to adopt, the very language of men," was only saying in other words what Dryden had said, and fighting the battle which Dryden had fought.[9]

Wordsworth's principle may have been revolutionary in his historical period through its contrast to eighteenth century practice, but the historical surge against tradition represented by Romantic poetics was also a return to the universal values of tradition in the absolute sense; it was a revolt against what had become traditional in the practical, historical sense only, a distinction fundamental to Eliot's critical thought.

Lewis Freed argued that Eliot preferred Wordsworth to Coleridge as a critic.[10] Perhaps it is Eliot's direct endorsement of Wordsworth on poetic diction that creates this impression, and Eliot's repetition of the doctrine's value, almost always referring to Wordsworth, in several essays. His purpose, I think, was to redirect appreciation of Wordsworth away from his Romantic elements to a more catholic and traditional view. The preference noted is not really one for

Wordsworth at all but for a particular poetic belief. Eliot divided critical activity into two sorts, one he called "essays of generalization," the other "appreciations of individual authors."[11] The second category held more promise for retaining general value beyond its historical period, Eliot believed. His writing on Wordsworth seems to classify him among the generalizers, one of great value, certainly, but limited. It is Coleridge whom Eliot ranks among the greatest critics of each category. As a general theorist, Coleridge, too, represents perhaps a few individual traditional values - his theory of imagination, for one. But he was also able to write criticism of individual authors and works that remained the most perceptive and provided the best understanding of them up to Eliot's time, as he believed. Coleridge, it appears, more justly represents "eternal value" than does Wordsworth in Eliot's system. When Eliot wrote about poetic diction, Wordsworth's name often appeared; Coleridge's name came into Eliot's discussions on many topics, and for more diverse purposes: Coleridge was held up as a warning against the dangers of metaphysical infringement on literary criticism, but he was also invoked as an authority on particular works, held up as the exemplum of the poet-critic, judged as a poet, and pitied as a man. Coleridge seems far more compatible with Eliot than does Wordsworth; Eliot appeared to have entered into the mind of Coleridge to gain full appreciation of his criticism; the mind of Wordsworth seems never to have been so inviting.

Eliot did not systematically single out the principles of Romantic criticism which he considered to be actually universal ideas. One must be guided by the frequency of his references to particular critics and their theories; Wordsworth, Coleridge, Goethe, and Poe were those most often cited. Eliot's treatment of Coleridge's criticism was more complex than his study of other critics; fewer ideas were dismissed, and a good deal of continuity of thought appears between the two. Coleridge represents the best possibility for accommodating Romanticism in tradition; Eliot's use of him critically and poetically will be discussed in a later section. His assessment of Poe is at first surprising: Eliot considered him among the first order of poet-critics. He rarely alluded to Poe in his essays and what few allusions occur are short and almost casual. The most concentrated source of Eliot's thought on Poe is a review, in the Nation and Athenaeum in May, 1927, of Israfel, a critical interpretation of Poe's poetry. One paragraph in Eliot's review stands out as an ostensible contradiction of his anti-Romantic stand:

> Poe was the direct heir of Byron . . . In following Byron, he was following the great tradition of English poetry in its Romantic phase. The Romantic phase was an essential phase, not only in England but for the whole of Europe. After the death of Byron it may be said that romanticism became diffused. Two men, and perhaps two men only, inherited the spirit of English romanticism: Poe and Heine. I should add Baudelaire, but Baudelaire is already influenced by Poe . . . In England the romantic cult was transformed by the enormous prestige of Tennyson; in America by Tennyson also and later by Whitman, the American Tennyson; in France by Victor Hugo and his contemporaries. But the true inheritors of the spirit of romanticism expressed by Byron (and spirit here implies spirituality) were Poe and Heine and Baudelaire. That is why these three poets are more modern today than any of their contemporaries: in preserving the spirit of romanticism they preserve the absolute spirit; they provide the explanation of romanticism and open the way to something else.[12]

This paragraph appears to have more positive remarks on and appreciation of Romanticism than Eliot was ever able to muster again. It is also one of the clearest examples of Eliot's critical process of detecting the universal elements in a particular artist's work or a particular period in literary history and judging its value to reside therein. Eliot called Romanticism a phase in "the great tradition," and limits true romanticism to that identified with the poetry of Byron and Poe. They appear as poets whose techniques, in that specific historical phase, were most representative of the universal values which comprise tradition. The particular manifestation of Romanticism exemplified by Byron was the "essential phase" for all of Europe, a comment that suggests, along with the reference to spirituality, that Eliot had the notion of the suffering, sinful self in mind and was concerned with a major mission he saw in art: the objective comtemplation of good and evil, which he praised as the great gift of Baudelaire. Poe's great insight was his aesthetic appreciation of the grotesque, the diseased, and the evil, not in themselves or for their gothic appeal, but in their relation to the whole of experience. Through his poetry and criticism, Poe allowed perception of the "absolute spirit." His work emphasized that seemingly antithetical phenomena could be united in an ideal whole. Along with Dante and Baudelaire, Poe demonstrated that, in Eliot's words, "the essential advantage for a poet is not, to have a beautiful world with which to deal: it is to be able to see beneath both beauty and ugliness; to see the boredom, and the horror, and the glory."[13] Perhaps it is in their ability to see a total order rather than disparate elements that Poe, Heine, and Baudelaire "provide the explanation of romanticism." As Eliot said in "Baudelaire," they mean something else. Their study of subjective experience is microcosmic, in contrast to the individualistic purposes of other

Romantic poets. They "open the way to something else," something beyond the individual and historical, into the universal. Historically, for Eliot, Romanticism led to the poetic inflation of Tennyson and the excessive emotion and deficient poetic expression of Whitman. It has value only within the larger framework of tradition, in its representative, universal elements.

Eliot further justified his sense of the universal quality of Poe as a poet-critic by considering Poe a "displaced European."[14] Eliot did not consider him part of an American tradition or even strictly of the English one. His view of Poe seems to contradict literary history, but Eliot was more interested in Poe's critical ideas than in his poetry: Eliot's view may have been based on Poe's theories and themes instead of on his poetic language and form. To Eliot, Poe is the fusion of the experience and techniques of several influences, and he passed them on in a manner that allowed for traditional coherence. Eliot seemed to consider him a great synthesizer, a view he expressed in "From Poe to Valéry." Poe's particularly significant critical achievement, Eliot claimed, was his recognition of the artistic force of "surprise" in poetry. Eliot allied this critical principle to the critical idea of Coleridge which stated that good poetry could make "the familiar strange, and the strange familiar." Eliot's reference placed Poe and Coleridge in the same critical company. In "Andrew Marvell," Eliot used the quality identified by Coleridge and Poe to explain the place of wit in poetic technique. Again, the value of the critical principle is its universal application, its historical context of Romanticism is irrelevant to its worth. In "Dante," Eliot again referred favorably to Poe's critical assessment of the quality of surprise in poetry, applying it this time to help explain in part how Dante achieved the emotional effect in the Brunetto Latini and Ulysses passages of the Inferno. One can see some similarity of theme in Dante, Villon, Coleridge, and Baudelaire with Poe; Eliot may have accorded Poe high standing as a poet-critic for his poetic treatment of the essential theme of good and evil, which he then expressed in general terms in his criticism.

Eliot's scattered remarks on Goethe and the essay "Goethe as the Sage," written late in Eliot's life, have a noticeably joyless air to them. For Eliot, enjoyment of a work of art comes after the full understanding of it; Eliot said he struggled with the works and ideas of Goethe for much of his life, putting off the reckoning for as long as he could. Possibly his comments on Goethe are diffuse, inconsistent, and ambivalent due to his feeling that Goethe represented an uncompleted academic assignment: so much guilt and work is involved that the promised pleasure appears dubious; relief from irritation is the more likely reward. Eliot's early judgment of Goethe in "What is a Classic?" was that he was limited as a poet to a Germanic sensibility, and his poetry was not classic because it could not be universal. He considered Faust to be too much unassimilated idea and not enough concentrated poetry. But Eliot encased his remarks in this vein between two essays whose common point is Goethe's universality. Eliot reviewed a critical work on the Romantics for the Athenaeum in 1919, generally agreeing with the author that the period was intellectually chaotic. But Eliot singled out Goethe as a mind unaffected by anarchy, calling him a representative of the Romantic movement because he was aware of the age. Eliot distinguished Goethe from the rest of the Romantics on the basis of his awareness because it implied a consciousness of relative and absolute values. Goethe was able to perceive his age as a phase, and indeed was instrumental in defining that phase for others, and yet he saw clearly its historical limitation in view of a larger and unifying order.

According to Eliot, "... through Goethe ... The Romantic Movement (I mean the Romantic Movement of these years, and not Romanticism in general) achieves the dignity of a phase in the changing personality of history."[15] One gets a sense again of Eliot's division between Romanticism the historical period and Romanticism the symbol, the former a category open to study for universal elements and the latter an ahistorical term of condemnation for its anti-traditional tendencies.

Eliot approved of Goethe as a poet-critic in the most generalized sense he ever used the term. While he disapproved of many of Goethe's literary works, he recognized the place of Faust in the ideal order of art: it inevitably affects our experience of Western literature. No education in the European tradition is complete without a knowledge of it, Eliot said in "Goethe as the Sage." Goethe's works in all their diversity proved the abundance, amplitude, and unity of his thought. Between the disapproving comments on Faust and Wilhelm Meister and the dearth of comments on Goethe's criticism, it is difficult to say that Eliot valued Goethe in more than theoretical terms. He did not name him as a great critic of either the generalizing or the specifically illuminating type. It seems to be Eliot's impression of how similar Goethe's mind was to Dante's and Shakespeare's in abstract qualities that made him finally place Goethe among the "great Europeans." Even without Eliot's having cited a specific poetic principle or critical insight made by Goethe, his perception makes of Goethe a poet-critic who embodied the values of tradition. By implication, those values include a recognition of the need to detect the signature of the absolute in each particular literary work and period, to affirm the value of the whole over the individual, and through one's poetry or criticism to impose the order of the Western tradition.

Goethe did not form part of that tradition as a Romantic poet or a Romantic critic, but as a representative thinker of a certain class of intellectual achievement, one whose nature is ahistorical.

The uniform qualities of the universal mind did not imply for Eliot uniformity of thought or belief, a point whose logical basis lies in his notion of the organicism of the ideal order of art. The more that body grows, the more we "know," as Eliot phrased it in "Tradition and the Individual Talent." Universal minds help to unite the new knowledge of art to the old order and in so doing serve to define and to preserve tradition. The best critics engage in this effort of separation, identifying the lasting from the temporary value. They may not be clear themselves of their function, or even about the criteria to be applied in the testing, and they may thus be great despite themselves, as Eliot depicted Wordsworth to be. Perhaps by way of excusing some errors of judgment Eliot admitted that "The critics of the romantic period were pioneers, and exhibit the fallibility of discoverers."[16] Later critics face the task of going through those discoveries to identify the valuable ideas and to assimilate them in current literary practice. Such work seems especially to demand the poet-critic's experience of criticism in the imaginative process. The poet-critic is a type of aesthetic translator; he refurbishes poetic theories to fit the style of his work and historical period. As Eliot pointed out about his own poetic theories, the aim was not to be "new" or "original," but to be useful to the poet and critic in clarifying what a good poem is, what it is made up of and how it is to be recognized. What the poet-critic "teaches" is the current state of our knowledge about ideal order. Each succeeding period "knows" more about literature because there is more literature behind it. Eliot as the critic separates the universal elements in

Romantic literature from the historical, and as the poetic theorist he reshapes Romantic poetic theory to serve the artistic needs of himself and his contemporaries. Eliot narrowed his focus of study to what he considered truly literary concerns; he dropped almost completely those Romantic theories which he considered to be the territory of philosophy, and metaphysics in particular, such as the concepts of Nature and transcendentalism. He took up Coleridge's theory of imagination to redefine it from his point of view, and he also discussed poetic issues related to Romantic psychology, in the form of aesthetic judgment, perception, and emotion.

The generalizing critic, the theorist, has in view at all times the question of how to recognize a great artistic work. Coleridge in Biographia Literaria and Eliot in the volumes of his critical essays studied the question from both ends, analyzing process and product alike. In terms of process, Eliot's conception of poetic imagination seems very much adapted from Coleridge, in a manner that repeats Eliot's treatment of other Romantic critics. His version of the theory of imagination basically accords with Coleridge's, in the powers attributed to the imaginative faculty, notably in its synthesizing function. Eliot rejected the distinction between fancy and imagination as a matter of semantics and faulty logic, and as a distinction possible in theory but "difficult to apply in practice."[17] Defining fancy as a "mode of memory," as Coleridge did, caused logical problems for Eliot; perhaps he wished to dispense with an issue that had by his time become one for the science of psychology. He admired Lowes' Road to Xanadu for illustrating the presence of memory in the imaginative process but considered the work to be "beyond the frontier of literary criticism."[18] Despite Coleridge's emphasis on the different qualities of fancy and imagination, and his careful correction of Wordsworth for confusing kind with degree, Eliot passed over the disagreement with something near to benign neglect, or tolerance for the eccentric. Coleridge's distinction seemed unnecessarily technical and overly complex to Eliot, since it led to the same conclusion that a careful critic would arrive at using his analytical powers and developed taste:

There is so much memory in imagination that if you are to distinguish between imagination and fancy in Coleridge's way you must define the difference between memory in imagination and memory in fancy . . . This distinction, in itself, need not give you distinct imagination and fancy, but only degrees of imaginative success.[19]

Eliot seemed intent on establishing a parochial view by discounting particular critical points that interfered with his sense of a unified theory of imagination throughout the English tradition. In his introduction to The Use of Poetry and the Use of Criticism, Eliot presented his argument for excluding the individual and historical content of criticism as a means of isolating the eternal element of poetry; he wished to try to understand "what does not change" through its contrast to "what is merely the expression of the spirit of an age."[20] Identifying the problems that criticism has addressed in each age is more valuable than studying its prescriptions, for the latter is the relative value and the former more likely to be the absolute. Coleridge's attempt to clarify fancy and imagination has value for Eliot as an indication of the imagination's essential importance to critical criteria; it has general value beyond its practical content. In the introduction, Eliot quoted first Dryden on fancy and imagination, and then Coleridge; after acknowledging differences in expression, background, and "developed state of mind," all due to the passage of time, Eliot stated, " . . . what we have to consider is, whether what we have here is two radically opposed theories of Poetic Imagination, or whether the two may be reconciled...."[21]

The tendency of all of Eliot's thought, in his essays and in his poetry, seems to be toward a positive assertion of that reconciliation's possibility. The impulse toward perception of an absolute order colors his criticism and poetry. In this instance, the impulse is evident first in Eliot's assimilation of Coleridge's theory of imagination. His criticism attempts to assimilate, not differentiate, ideas. Also, the specific idea in Coleridge's theory which he chooses to emphasize - the synthetic power of the poet as the root of creation - demonstrates the analytic and synthetic abilities of the critic to identify eternal elements and to construct a view of the Western literary tradition. In The Still Point, Ethel F. Cornwell notes the connection:

> Coleridge anticipated Eliot's use of the imagination to amalgamate 'disparate experience'; fuse thought and feeling, the perceiver and the perceived; and, like Eliot, sought the Divine through a recognition of the One in the Many, the eternal in the temporal. His emphasis upon intuition and revelation is echoed in the writing of Eliot . . . as is his insistence upon the 'law of polarity' and the reconciliation of opposites. . . .[22]

In "Andrew Marvell," Eliot quoted Coleridge's definition of imagination as a process of synthesizing to prove the greatness of "To His Coy Mistress." The preeminence of the synthetic imagination in Coleridge's critical thought in itself justifies Eliot's selective approval of his poetic theories and emancipates the idea from its Romantic context. In a similar way, Eliot adapted Coleridge's definition of creation and erased the division between pleasure and truth as aims of poetry.

In "The Frontiers of Criticism," Eliot defined his concept of creation very simply: "When the poem has been made, something new has happened, something that cannot be wholly explained by <u>anything that went before</u>. That, I believe, is what we mean by 'creation'."[23] In very general terms, Eliot's definition accords with a Romantic definition of creation derived from Leibniz and Kant. The new poem has a unique existence; it differs intrinsically from other poems even of the same type. Eliot was unwilling, however, to find value purely in originality, an unwillingness which implicitly refutes transcendental idealism. A work of art must be individual and yet it must still conform to the external structure of tradition in Eliot's view. If the scope of the Romantic concept of creation is limited to literary application, however, and if it is taken as an element of, and not a whole, poetic theory, then it can be reconciled with Eliot's definition. Should the question arise, is the concept still a Romantic one, its answer is a justification of the process: the universal part of the historical theory is what is left, and the true value of it thus appears. Eliot carefully defined the role of pleasure as a criterion of a poem's worth so that creativity remained a conceivably measurable element in the poem itself, not in the perception of the reader:

> To understand a poem comes to the same thing as to enjoy it for the right reasons. One might say that it means getting from the poem such enjoyment as it is capable of giving: to enjoy a poem under a misunderstanding as to what it is, is to enjoy what is merely a projection of our own mind.[24]

There is little question that Eliot considered the poem and the projection as completely unrelated entities. His theory of the objective correlative is antithetical to Romantic theories of the perception of art. But insofar as he recognized pleasure as an end of poetry, and "truth" as a term irrelevant to evaluation, Eliot agreed with Coleridge, a generalization for the sake of continuity.

When Eliot used the term "psychology," he seemed to wish to evoke a sense of the word's root meaning. He called Baudelaire and Racine "the greatest two psychologists, the most curious explorers of the soul."[25] If one takes "psychologists" and "soul" in this quotation as literary terms (as Eliot most likely used them), the probable reference is to each poet's presentation of human struggles with an absolute order; it is unlikely in this context that "psychologists" refers to a field of scientific inquiry. How far Romantic psychology, especially as it appears in Coleridge's criticism (for it is his work which Eliot names as the beginning of a relationship between literary studies and psychology) is a scientific, pseudo-scientific, or philosophical pursuit, and how far it is metaphoric vocabulary for a description of the imaginative process, determines Eliot's attitude towards its theories. How the mind works on the data of experience is a valid question in Eliot's system if one wishes to know how a work of art is more than individual expression. For Eliot, theorizing about perception, imagination, and expression to promote and defend subjective judgment is a non-literary pursuit that subordinates art to idea. No work of art can be truly successful if "instead of thinking with our feelings (a very different thing) we corrupt our feelings with ideas; we produce the political, the emotional idea, evading sensation and thought."[26] This quotation is from Eliot's essay "Henry James," in which he praises James for being "like the best French critics in maintaining a point of view, a viewpoint untouched by the parasite idea."[27] Were the Romantic theory of imagination not so definitively tied to a transcendental notion of perception, were it untouched by parasite philosophy, it would not be so alien to Eliot's sense of the imagination. He did not reject Wordsworth's theory of recollection absolutely, citing it instead as an "inexact formula." That imagination works on individual perception, and from that point proceeds to the production of a new entity, is a theory evident even in "Tradition and the Individual Talent." What Eliot seemed to question is the aesthetic judgment of that entity in subjective terms, for if one does not impose objective standards on the new work of art, one cannot determine its real value. Eliot suspected the effect of subjective standards to be a loss of relativity between the self and reality, a psychological breakdown, as he defined "psychological." Eliot viewed this process as historically manifest: "What I see, in the history of English poetry, is not so much daemonic possession as the splitting up of personality."[28] "The Waste Land" incorporates the same idea poetically.

The importance of the relation of the product of imagination to real experience and the artistic inauthenticity of the fantastic idea, the idea that does not extend beyond the individual mind, is evident in one of Eliot's rare comments on the novel:

If you examine some of Dostoevsky's most successful, most imaginative "flights," you find them to be projections, continuations, of the actual, the observed . . . his point of departure is always a human brain in a human environment, and the "aura" is simply the continuation of the quotidian experience of the brain into seldom explored extremities of torture. Because most people are too unconscious of their own suffering to suffer much, this continuation appears fantastic . . . in Balzac the fantastic element is of another sort: it is not an extension of reality, it is an atmosphere thrown upon reality direct from the personality of the writer.[29]

The theory of the objective correlative precludes critical acceptance of a work that is fantastic in a personal way only. Eliot's theory was perhaps intended to correct an error of overgeneralization made by the pioneering Romantic critics. Romantic theories about the nature of the self represented to Eliot a "progress in self-consciousness," attributable to Coleridge, Wordsworth, Carlyle, Hartley, Kant, Leibniz, and Locke, according to Cornwell as she interprets Peckham, who suggested that Coleridge's "dynamic organicism" was a rudimentary theory of the unconscious.[30] Cornwell made the distinction that "the Romantics placed it outside and above, whereas we conceive of the unconscious as inside and underneath."[31] Eliot's approach to Romanticism, and to criticism in general, can be viewed in part as the correction of what to him was an historical error: " . . . the study of psychology has impelled men . . . to investigate the mind of the poet with a confident ease which has led to some fantastic excesses and aberrant criticism . . . ."[32] He could dismiss the transcendental aspect of Romantic poetry and criticism as outdated theory, a part of intellectual history superseded by theories reflecting the greater knowledge of later ages, and still retain Coleridge's theory of the imagination in truncated form. Eliot's comment, "The great artists do not unite imagination with observation," divorced the creative process from the psychological function of perception, perhaps not so much in the nature of the two activities as in the critical interest of each.[33]

Together with Coleridge, Eliot supported the primacy and integrity of poetic language. Both agreed with Wordsworth, but to a point: poetic diction should be natural. However, the poet achieves a natural effect in his poetry not by adopting "the very language of men" but by recreating it: representation over copy, poetry over prose. Coleridge and Eliot alike insisted on the "<u>essential</u> difference between the language of prose and of metrical composition."[34] Poetry for both is its own order of thought. Eliot held an apparently more radical belief in the unique abilities of poetry than even Coleridge claimed, although Eliot seemed anxious to insist on its unique nature so no other thought could encroach upon it, while Coleridge calmly proceeded with poetry's encroachment on a variety of disciplines. Each poet-critic believed in the organic unity of a poem as an essential and critical principle, one that helped define poetry and assess its greatness. Most of that critical theory which Eliot found to be nearly irreconcilable with his ideas resided in Coleridge's poetry, whose ideas Eliot apparently judged to be at odds with the poet's prose works. Eliot devoted his critical thought to topics he judged to be truly literary by consciously limiting his discussions despite their implications for philosophical issues, as he did at the end of "Tradition and the Individual Talent": "This essay proposes to halt at the frontier of metaphysics or mysticism, and confine itself to such practical conclusions as can be applied by the responsible person interested in poetry."[35] The proposal follows his discussion of the nature of imaginative activity, in which the "platinum" mind of the poet is in a state of extreme concentration, a state which "does not happen consciously or of deliberation."[36] The actual transmutation of the artist's experience into an objective work of art, the instance of creation itself, remains as mysterious and unknowable in Eliot's theory as it was in any deep, romantic chasm. In <u>Poetry and Belief in the Work of T.S. Eliot</u>, Kristian Smidt noted the presence of an uncharacteristic sense of the super-rational in Eliot's theory of the artistic process:

> . . . at one stage in the creative process something mysterious seems to happen, which Eliot can only explain by means of a chemical comparison . . . In introducing his notion of "intensity of the artistic process, Eliot seems to approach a kind of aesthetic mysticism. The most important moment in the creation of a poem is removed from the sphere of reason and familiar emotions and transferred to a special artistic faculty which can only be known by its effects . . . Eliot, it must be admitted, comes close to accepting the idea of supernatural inspiration.[37]

However much Eliot disliked the Romantic poet, his notion of a perfect critic, a poet-critic, who perceived universal values and who produced work which transcended his historical confines, provided a theoretical means of reconciling Romanticism with tradition. The movement itself could be treated as a part of literary history; those works which were in harmony with tradition the critic could consider valuable without accepting their Romantic context. The theory of universality, of "representative men," could be used to explain Coleridge, Wordsworth, Goethe, Poe, even, perhaps, Emerson, as traditional thinkers. By focusing on the universal ideas in the critics and theorists of the age, Eliot could posit a literary continuity, if not a purely poetic one. It seems that Eliot addressed Romanticism positively in critical terms, and was able to demonstrate traditional coherence in specific critical theories and values. In "The Waste Land," Romantic echoes and allusions suggest that Eliot also found a way to synthesize his sense of Romanticism's presence in the Western Tradition of poetry, and the ability of tradition to assimilate its anti-traditional forces.

CHAPTER FIVE:

"TRADITION AND THE INDIVIDUAL TALENT" AND "THE WASTE LAND":
CRITICAL AND POETIC CORRESPONDENCE

The theme of a search for unity that pervades Eliot's poetic and critical works may be taken as a guiding principle in the study of his art and thought. His impulse to reconcile seemingly discrete orders of thought is most apparent in his treatment of the poet and critic. In Eliot's system, the appearance of disorder and contradiction in literary history may be refined through a rarefying (or transcendent) theory of tradition, which leaves the facts of history intact but removes meaning from the historical level and assigns it instead to the unrestricted realm of the universal. Eliot could reject the anti-traditional elements in the work of a particular artist as non-literary ideas and treat the remainder as the essential material. The assumed division in the nature of poetry and criticism may be surmounted through the figure of the poet-critic, who performs objective evaluations of literature for both poetic and critical ends, thereby creating a reciprocal relationship of poetic and critical ideas. In the case of Eliot, an equivalence of poetic and critical belief appears as a conscious intention, an actual precept in the body of his work. It is most evident in his discussion of the poet-critic, his isolation of equivalent qualities in the "Great European" and the "Classic," and his belief that modern poetry must be critical poetry. A further parallel may be made between the critical ideas of "Tradition and the Individual Talent" and the poetic concerns of "The Waste Land"; finally, one can read "The Waste Land" itself in one way as a poem that corrects

Romantic theory and reinforces tradition. It is at once a critical and poetic effort to reintegrate the disparate endeavors and beliefs found in Western literature.

In critical practice, the assumption that the criticism of a particular author guides the composition of his artistic works does not always hold true, despite Eliot's argument. Belief in the equation of artistic and critical ideas may have the pernicious effect of tempting the critic to reduce poetic language to factual discourse by explicating a poem in terms of the poet's critical tenets. But in the case of Eliot, his repeated insistence on the need to consider a poet's criticism in terms of his poetry, and his poetry in light of his criticism, suggests not a means of explication so much as a literary theory of relativity. Eliot considered the best criticism to be "workshop" criticism, criticism which came out of the early stages of the artistic process. According to Eliot, the critical mind of the poet working on the material of his poem most likely will produce critical insights that reveal not only the artistic intent of the poet in a specific poem but will also demonstrate a useful analytical method of determining the poetic from the non-poetic. Criticism developed as part of poetic activity will have proved its ability to be used effectively in artistic assessment by having been an integral part of poetic creation. The literary worth of the author's work will be a kind of check on the value of the criticism as well: if the poem is judged to be good, then the critical work that went into it must have value. The poetry of a poet-critic determines the value of his criticism, and his criticism in turn supports the poetic process, as Eliot claimed: "My criticism has this in common with that of Ezra Pound, that its merits and its limitations can be fully appreciated only when it is considered in relation to the poetry I have written myself," and that the "poetic critic is criticizing poetry in order to create poetry."[1] Eliot viewed the best criticism to be essentially a part of poetry, inherently related in meaning to the poetry it serves. The poetry and criticism of a poet-critic reflect common beliefs, despite different means of expression and different scopes of meaning.

None of Eliot's comments on this issue suggests that criticism limits poetry in a directly normative way. In keeping with the theory of tradition, his idea of criticism is that it serves to maintain a connection between the new creation and earlier literary works. The critical sense of the objective critic comes from intensive study, that of the poet-critic from the same study but also from his poetic sensibility. His criticism reflects objective thought and incorporates influences as well, as Eliot claimed was the case with his own criticism. In this way, the critical work occurring as part of the imaginative process represents tradition, causing the new work to exist from its inception in implicit relation to tradition.

On this level, criticism can control poetry at one point in the creation of it, and it is in this sense that there is an equivalence of meaning in a poet's criticism and poetry. The critical and the poetic expression reveal a certain belief about the nature of art. The worth of that belief resides in the work of art; it must be judged against tradition first, and its value then determines the value of the criticism: "What the poet writes about poetry . . . must be assessed in relation to the poetry he writes."[2] The emphasis which this point receives in Eliot's criticism underscores his sense of the primary nature of poetry: poetry determines tradition; criticism reinforces it, both in its place in the imaginative process and in its use for objective assessment of a given work of art. The poet-critic's achievement in the realm of poetry and tradition - the work in itself and as part of tradition - gives authority to his criticism.

If one acknowledges the artistic worth of an author's work, one implicitly acknowledges the worth of his critical works as well, as Eliot argued in the case of Swinburne: "The author of Swinburne's critical essays is also the author of Swinburne's verse: if you hold the opinion that Swinburne was a very great poet, you can hardly deny him the title of a great critic."[3] The equivalence in worth rests on Eliot's belief that it is a logical impossibility for the great artist to embody divergent and inconsistent ideas about art: "If such views are held about art, it follows that 'a fortiori' whoever holds them must hold similar views about criticism."[4] The equivalence of the views logically follows because Eliot held that the criticism of poets had the major intention of defending the kind of poetry they wrote, or of helping them to formulate the kind they wished to write. Thus Eliot endorsed a belief in an essential tie between critical ideas and poetic practice in the work of the great artist. In the case of specific Romantic poets, one can see the basis for Eliot's apparently disunified view of Romantic criticism and poetry. The disparity in his estimation of Wordsworth and Coleridge as critics and then as poets may be accounted for by his emphasis on certain theories in their criticism as universally valid; their poetry, however, was created without such selectivity, and therefore it embodies not only universal elements but erroneous theories related to subjectivism as well. Coleridge's tendency to include non-literary ideas in his criticism reflects the same tendency of his poetry: each is limited and marred by metaphysics. But unlike critical discourse, the nature of poetic language makes selective acceptance virtually impossible. Consequently, Eliot rejected most of the poetry of Wordsworth and Coleridge, even as he endorsed some of their major poetic theories.

The need for equivalence in poetic and critical thought appears again in Eliot's emphasis on the critical nature of modern poetry. As Sean Lucy observed in T.S. Eliot and the Idea of Tradition, Eliot located in poetry, from the time of Wordsworth and Shelley especially, a need to address critical questions about the nature and form of poetry in poetry itself.[5] He believed the modern period in Western literature to be an age of inextricable poetry and criticism. Eliot notes a modern demand on the critic that he have "a creative interest, a focus upon the immediate future. The important critic is the person who is absorbed in the present problems of art, and who wishes to bring the forces of the past to bear upon the solution of these problems."[6] The modern critic's criticism exists as a tie between present and traditional poetic practice in its immediate relevance. In poetry, the same concern is revealed in the effort to document the poetic process through the inclusion of critical questions. "The Waste Land" creates with its system of allusions a vision of tradition, and represents a combined critical and poetic attempt to unite modern poetry with it.

Eliot's proviso that a poet's criticsm be read in relation to his poetry seems to be an effort to assure proper interpretation, not necessarily of a specific poem, but of an aesthetic idea. The expression of the idea in a critical work is complemented by its incorporation in poetic works. Such dual expression clarifies its import and implications, and one has not fully comprehended the idea if one has not considered it in its prose and poetic forms, in theory and in practice. "The Solitary Reaper," for example, expresses poetically the theories of natural diction amd common subject discussed in Wordsworth's Preface. The ideas are present in the language and imagery of the poem; they make up part of its form and meaning. When Eliot wrote, ". . . I do not believe that my own criticism has had, or could have had, any influence whatever apart from my own poems," he implied a congruence of meaning between the critical works and the poems, and a dependence of the former on the latter for elucidation and completion.[7]

The ideas of "Tradition and the Individual Talent," if they were taken in isolation fromn Eliot's poetry, might suggest a call for literary conservatism to the point of reactionary form and content, and Eliot might appear to be a twentieth-century Parnassian. But when the essay is read in relation to "The Waste Land" - the poem that seems to deal most directly with the idea of tradition - the poetic implications of the critical theory are shown to be unrestrictive in form, diction, subject, and attitude towards art. There may be a shock in store for the reader who encounters Eliot's essays first, "The Waste Land" second: Eliot's usually formal language, conservative ideas, and cautionary tone in his essays do not prepare one for the atrocities, in language and subject, of the poem. But despite the seemingly very different intentions of his essay and poem, further examination of them produces a sense of coherence, and helps to illustrate how the density of poetic language and complexity of poetic form make poetry the ultimate vehicle for an aesthetic theory, an idea about art, and criticism a utilitarian outline of it.

"The Waste Land," published in final form three years after the publication of "Tradition and the Individual Talent," may be treated as the poetic equivalent of the ideas presented in that critical work. It cannot be overemphasized that this equivalence refers to a single level of meaning in the poem and is not meant as a comprehensive reading of it. What I suggest is that part of the poem (not in the sense of specific lines but complexity of meaning) is a treatment of tradition and the effects of anti-traditional beliefs. The theory of ideal order finds expression in part of the structure of the poem, that of tradition mainly as a dominant theme. Individuality and impersonality, the subjective versus the universal, also form a major theme, one that relates directly to the theory of the impersonality of the artist in the same essay.

Eliot's discussion of ideal order among works of art does not depict that order as an historical structure, but the theory does rest on a notion of chronology. Changes to the structure occur not in sequence, however, but as simultaneous modification, signifying the organic relationship between the "monuments," as Eliot referred to the artistic works which comprise ideal order. The great work of art is above history and must be judged finally in the context of pre-existing monuments. Recognized as a principle of evaluation, "ideal order" maintains a standard for art which prevents historical errors of judgment and provides a perspective from which to view the work in its universal relevance. In "The Waste Land," allusions to the monuments abound, but the speaker "can connect / Nothing with nothing."[8] The works of art that embody our cultural tradition are present in the poem in a fragmentary way only, not in ideal order; in fact, there is no order, no coherence in their presence. They appear as historical fragments, textual fragments, characters and images torn from not only their original context but from the unifying system of the ideal order of Western tradition. "Elizabeth and Leicester / Beating oars" do not evoke the Renaissance but a modern La Pia, "Supine on the floor of a narrow canoe." Line 202, "Et O ces voix d'enfants, chantant dans la coupole," from Verlaine's "Parsifal," no longer shows the triumph of innocence, but goes unheard between scenes of sexual decadence, from Mrs. Porter to Mr. Eugenides. In lines 243-46, Tiresias attempts to impose a context:

> (And I Tiresias have foresuffered all
> Enacted on this same divan or bed;
> I who have sat by Thebes below the wall
> And walked among the lowest of the dead.)

The parenthetical expression demonstrates the questionable relevance of his observation. Images juxtaposing ancient and modern cultural centers, as in lines 375-77:

> Jerusalem Athens Alexandria
> Vienna London
> Unreal

suggest an alienation so great that any sense of continuity is beyond conception.

Representative works from almost every age of literature since the Greek myths appear, but without a chronological framework. The "monuments" still exist, but no one can see beyond them as immediate particulars in order to detect their value. Discontinuity seems to take the place of history in the poem; the historical ages of glory that are depicted seem to be isolated, frozen moments that are unrelated to later ages, as in the Elizabethan image. There is discontinuity in geography among the various speakers and their memories, and no culture retains a sense of itself, a condition represented even more strongly in the discontinuity of language, the basic identifying principle of a culture and its art. Instead of ideal order among works of art, a system of decadent relation takes it place, in which works of art appear in connection to inanities, a connection that promotes mutual devaluation:

> O City city, I can sometimes hear

> Beside a public bar in Lower Thames Street,
>
> The pleasant whining of a mandoline
>
> And a clatter and a chatter from within
>
> Where fishmen lounge at noon: where the walls
>
> Of Magnus Martyr hold
>
> Inexplicable splendour of Ionian white and gold.

Cathedrals and Greek art are physically present, but they are symbolically empty: the "fishmen" see no more than their "public bar." The theory of ideal order is present in the poem only by implication: without its recognition as an entity above history and as a standard of judgment, no sense of order or value can exist. To fail to recognize it is to lose a sense of the value of the past and thus to be blind to value in the present. While Eliot narrowed the application of the theory as it appears in "Tradition and the Individual Talent" to literary evaluation expressly, in his poem it is an unrestricted element of structural meaning.

The purpose of a theory of ideal order in Eliot's criticism is to provide a standard for a sense of tradition and a means to its preservation. Most of his critical thought seems to be centered on a belief in the necessity of tradition. One would then expect that Eliot's poetry would incorporate the same concern, since he claimed that the sources of his criticism were intertwined with his poetic beliefs and practice. The "Sweeney" poems and "The Waste Land" embody the critical concept of tradition through their organization by contrast of modern and ancient, a blunt juxtaposition of values: Sweeney and the clerk/typist versus Agamemnon and Tiresias. The Greek monuments stand but are in isolation from the present culture, which has lost its awareness of the unity of the past. Attempts to reconstruct past order are so undirected by any guiding principle that the end of "The Waste Land" is a patchwork of relics whose significance is unclear, a confusion of Western relics and Eastern philosophy. From the first allusion to the final images of helplessness, and the comprehensive vision of Tiresias throughout, the state of Western tradition seems to be one of the poem's unifying themes. The poem also seems to place itself within tradition by its allusions, performing poetically what the critic would do through direct comparison and analysis.

Eliot's theory of tradition, as it is explained in his essay and expressed in his poem, bears some resemblance to Erich Auerbach's idea of "figura," especially as Auerbach interprets Dante's use of it. Both "figura" and "tradition" emphasize individual worth within an encompassing and deeply significant system. Auerbach's argument that, "For Dante the literal meaning or historical reality of a figure stands in no contradiction to its profounder meaning, but precisely 'figures' it; the historical reality is not annulled, but confirmed and fulfilled by the deeper meaning," suggests a relative system of values similar to Eliot's argument that a true work of art has individual worth, but for it to be individual, it must have meaning in relation to ideal order as well.[9] Eliot called his critical system "a judgment, a comparison, in which two things are measured by each other . . . We say: a new work appears to conform, and is perhaps individual, or it appears individual, and may conform; but we are hardly likely to find that it is one and not the other."[10] The allusions in "The Waste Land" force on the reader the sense of a wider context than the author's historical period; they summon a sense of the poem's relation to the past. The various speakers in the poem lack consciousness of that deeper meaning and wider context in the poem as they attempt to unite past and present experience. The allusions conjure up not only the individual works of the past, but through them the idea of a unified tradition.

The third major critical precept of "Tradition and the Individual Talent" is the impersonality of the artist, a doctrine that is the antithesis of a subjective theory of art. In Eliot's view, the artist undergoes a "surrender of himself as he is at the moment to something which is more valuable." The "self-sacrifice" of the artist parallels a theme common to Eliot's poems and basic to his appreciation of poets such as Dante and Baudelaire: perception of worth comes through an understanding of relativity, a recognition that the particular implies the universal. A work of art takes precedence over the personality of the artist and reveals its ultimate worth in the realm of ideal order. In "The Waste Land," the suffering of individual voices is unrelenting; reality seen from the individual perspective is pain-filled, confused, and apparently meaningless: "I could not / Speak, and my eyes failed, I was neither / Living nor dead, and I knew nothing." To search for meaning in a realm of time and decay is to invite frustration and, finally, apathy.

The conditions of daily existence in the individual, temporal world must be placed in a larger context, a unified system, if one is to achieve understanding and deliverance. A spiritual equivalent of depersonalization appears as a theme in the poem. Personal feelings and individual values must be sacrificed to a larger good; one must first be able to recognize and accept the notion of the larger good before one can escape through art or some form of spiritual transcendence. The fragments of consciousness in "The Waste Land" are disunified on even an individual level, and seem no longer able to conceive a notion of unity. They display a generalized feeling of desire, a discomforting yearning, a sifting among the ruins of culture with an uneasy sense of mystified attraction reminiscent of another system of correspondence, Baudelaire's lines, "L'homme y passe à travers des forêts de symboles / Qui l'observent avec des regards familiers."[11] In "The Waste Land," a sense of external meaning persists through the end of the poem. At the end, it is unclear which has been lost, the misery of purely subjective experience, or passage to the ordered realm of universal values. As in the essay, the poem emphasizes that escape from individuality is the only means of attaining a sense of worth.

By relying again on Eliot's advice to consider his poetry in relation to his criticism, one can read "The Waste Land" as a poem about the preservation of tradition and as an attempt to re-establish the awareness and the practice of traditional poetry. In his critical essays, Eliot specified Romanticism as an unorthodox part of Western literature, and Romantic poetry as antipathetic to traditional standards. One can see in the poem a parallel treatment of Romanticism and its effects within the spheres of cultural and spiritual life. The images of past epochs and allusions to artistic works up to the era of Romanticism depict a world of sacrifice and redemption, passion and fertility. Scenes from modern times and allusions to post-Romantic works form the major images of loss, waste, and despair. The Romantic age lies between the two worlds; Romanticism seems to be the point of transition from a world of organic unity to a world of cultural disarray and spiritual death. Eliot used the ages of literary history as a metaphor for the cycle of birth, suffering, and rebirth that is the foundation of his view of human life. Unless artists reassert their relation to tradition by abandoning subjective standards in favor of the universal values inherent in ideal order, Eliot seems to imply, art cannot retain its value. "The Waste Land" seems to state poetically how and why Romanticism conflicts with tradition and inevitably weakens it. The poem forces the issue of Romanticism and its relation to tradition, just as the critical essays do. "The Waste Land" seems a poetic correction of Romantic influence through its depiction of Romanticism's negative effects.

In "The Waste Land," the place of Romanticism in tradition is clarified through its contrast to other periods of literature. The allusions in the poem help to create an historical framework for its generally disjointed structure. Up to a certain era, each literary age is represented by an image that suggests the particular spiritual cohesion of that age. The figure of Tiresias, whom Eliot designated as the center of the poem, represents the inception of the Western tradition in Greek antiquity. According to Eliot's note, Tiresias unites what is "seen" in the separate scenes of the poem; he may be taken as the symbol of necessary consciousness of the process of suffering, regeneration, and rebirth. The historical basis of the poem begins with the images drawn from the work of Weston and Frazer. They represent the pagan era, as Weston, Frazer, and Eliot interpret it, an age of unarticulated and perhaps unconscious urges to observe rituals of birth, death, and rebirth. Later, the Greek tradition added a mythological expression of the impulse to renewal. The myths and literature of the two ages emphasized self-sacrifice for what was then an integrated spiritual and physical reward. As a figure of antiquity, Tiresias is the literary equivalent of the cultural tradition: he is like the sacrificed god of both pagans and Christians. He consorts with his gods, he combines sexual regeneration metaphorically in his dual sexual lives, and he is witness to the self-sacrifice of Oedipus in service to the continued existence of his people's spiritual life. At the same time, Tiresias and the sybil connect beginning and end of the era through their visionary power and their ultimate decay and exhaustion. Biblical references complete a depiction of the ancient framework. The Judeo-Christian age, represented in the poem through allusions and imagery drawn from the Old and New Testaments, replaces the scattered pagan creeds and asserts a religious basis for rebirth.

A slight echo of Yeats's "The Second Coming" sounds in the poem as this new age begins its cycle. Augustine offers the first warnings of apocalypse: the city will be the new place of destruction: "To Carthage then I came / Burning burning burning burning." At the end of the poem, the swallow image from "Pervigilium Veneris" prefigures the coming alienation of man from nature, and thus from his desire for rebirth. The figure of Dante looms over the age, a kind of hope for unification of past faith and modern life; his poem might guide mankind to the path of resurrection. Allusions to the medieval romances, especially to Tristan and Isolde and Parsifal, reflect the unity of passion, suffering, and religious faith. Renaissance images of rebirth appear in several references; The Tempest especially emphasizes death and resurrection. Images from Paradise Lost show the unifying concern with evil and redemption. Weakening classical and Christian influence finally appears in the song taken from Goldsmith's Vicar of Wakefield. It shows a moral system taken over by sentimentality, in which the strength and will to sacrifice the self is fueled more by manners than by spiritual awareness. By this point, the spiritual has been made material, the first step in its degradation and, ultimately, its imperceptibility.

At this point in the historical framework of the poem, direct allusions to periods of literary history lapse. The historical framework does not reappear until we see whole lines from Baudelaire, Nerval, and Verlaine, quoted in the original. The Symbolist presence is so strong that it underlines a Romantic absence; Symbolism's full representation seems a reaction against a negative influence. Some great loss has occurred between the era of Goldsmith's song and Baudelaire's accusation and despair, and that loss seems to be a loss of knowledge, awareness, daring, and sacrifice, which transforms the fertile life into the waste. By implication, Romantic aesthetic and philosophical bases in subjectivism seem to disrupt the human connection with an established social and cultural order. Reliance on the ego and transcendental will destroy former ties of responsibility, accountability, and community. Self-sacrifice turns into experiential exploration; for Eliot, such exploration can lead only to a trap, a closed cell. In the poem, no images of regeneration or rebirth come from Romantic creeds. Romanticism creates selfish, insular, sterile offspring. It destroys the sense of cohesive culture by undercutting classical values or objective views of the world. The historical framework of the poem, by leaving Romanticism out, indicts the nineteenth century as the turning point for Western culture: the Romantic age acts as a catalyst for turn-of-the-century despair and alienation.

Because Eliot observed his own requirement that the critic be erudite, the lack of specific Romantic allusions in "The Waste Land" must be attributed to a poetic motive, not a critical shortcominmg. Romanticism is absent by design, a design that may indicate that the lack of a direct Romantic presence in the poem is integral to its meaning overall. The content of "The Waste Land" has an aura of inclusiveness, a sense of comprehensiveness provoked by suggestion, allusion, and selective representation. The poem may be read as a history of our cultural tradition. The major speaker, Tiresias, has an inclusive consciousness of ancient and modern, male and female, pagan and Christian. The final image of "fragments shored against our ruin," representing on one level the greatest literary works of the Western tradition, suggests a structure of concerted efforts, all of which once formed a cohesive whole. No Romantic fragment appears among the ruins: Romanticism is left out of the poem perhaps because it was itself outside of cultural coherence. It could not be included because it did not conform. The divorce of Romanticism from tradition creates part of the poem's tension. Eliot used Romantic imagery very like that found in Coleridge's poetry to illustrate the error and danger of Romanticism: instead of transcendence, it produced negation of former modes of life and art. Its legacy is a pervasive sense of no escape, no movement, and no immediate hope of rebirth. Organized religion disintegrates; cities become underworlds where cultural relics go unrecognized and natural feeling is extinguished; and without stimulation from culture or nature, the human will to act is dissipated, and man embarks on an age of lifelessness.

Eliot's criticism of Romanticism was at this point as negative as his depiction of it in the poem; the actual critical work of justifying Romanticism as part of tradition came later. But the solution was prefigured in "The Waste Land" through the use of Coleridge as the representative of Romantic poetry and thought. In Eliot's critical essays, Coleridge as a poet-critic formed the major connection between Romanticism and traditional poetic theory. Given Eliot's belief in the continuity of an artist's critical and poetic works, one might expect a similar use of Coleridge in "The Waste Land." The multiple references to Coleridge in the essays, both the admiring and the chastising comments, indicate that Eliot depended on Coleridge to symbolize the historical period of Romanticism, that for him Coleridge was a representative Romantic in addition to his standing as a poet-critic beyond the temporal bounds of literary history. Perhaps Eliot's many references to Coleridge in his essays have overshadowed the presence of Coleridge's poetry in "The Waste Land."

That Coleridge's work does enter into Eliot's may seem unlikely for at least two reasons. First, Eliot's allusions are for the most part either direct (actual lines or names of characters, for example), or they are specifically footnoted, yet no direct reference to Coleridge appears. Next, Eliot seemed more interested in Coleridge as a critic than as a poet, and logically one might dismiss Coleridge's influence on Eliot as a minor point. Coleridge seems outside of Eliot's intellectual heritage because his Romantic philosophy directly violated Eliot's literary theory, especially as he outlined it in "Tradition and the Individual Talent," by imposing the self, the senses, and nature as the absolute values for art. The implications of Romanticism for Eliot were decadence, egotism, moral passivity, and anti-traditional thought, all of which describe the waste land itself, as an image in poetry and as a mirror of culture in general. Coleridge's view of nature must have appeared to Eliot as a system of perverted feeling and fraudulent knowledge; Coleridge's poetry embodied that system and so may have come to characterize for Eliot a warped, subjective view of life and art. That perception of Coleridge, at any rate, characterizes Eliot's poetic usage of him in "The Waste Land."

Coleridge appears in the poem through Eliot's allusions to his poems and to his philosophy both in specific lines and in organizing themes. Eliot did not note the use of Coleridge's poems directly, as he did with other sources, but they appear as sub-texts to "The Waste Land" nonetheless: they form the viewpoint that Eliot treats as one cause of the modern waste land, both in their own meaning and in their place in literary history. Perhaps the very lack of specific citation represents Eliot's acknowledgement of the force and influence of Coleridge's poetry, as well as his judgment on their human and artistic consequences. Coleridge was an "almost great" poet in Eliot's estimation, not an equal of Dante, nor of Shakespeare. No line of Coleridge's poetry could in Eliot's poem bear a weight equal to the weight borne by quotations from the two earlier poets. But the "near greatness" of Coleridge's poetry makes it a traditional force, irreversibly altering the past, and influencing the poet of the present. Coleridge, and Romanticism, are part of Western tradition, a logical difficulty since in some ways Romanticism denies that culture, at least in Eliot's view, by drawing so much of its content from that which is outside the tradition, while rejecting much of the content of Western culture.

Eliot's theory of tradition allowed for and emphasized the need for the "really new," but what entered tradition with the Romantics was a theme of cultural rebellion, a questioning and often rejection of what came before. The poetic theories of Wordsworth and Shelley, the new forms that Wordsworth and Coleridge advocated and in some cases practiced, and the philosophy of Rousseau are Eliot's specific citations of sources of disorder in tradition. One might extend the list to the German Romantic critics; all seemed to be untraditional in Eliot's view because they ignored the order formed by the past. Their standards consisted of locating their contemporary values in past works and judging the past exclusively in terms of the present, thereby eclipsing the past's authority. To Romantic critics, Homer and Shakespeare met the standards of naturalness and originality; Pope and his age, however were to be ejected from the new "order." But the literary values determined by such a system of self-reference cannot have universal relevance, and must finally engender disorder.

Since the end of an era does not end its influence, according to Eliot's system, the danger of Romantic standards continued beyond the Romantic age. To halt its continuing influence, Eliot and the French Symbolists rejected Romanticism, but they could not excise it from tradition. For Eliot especially it represented a devastating influence. It interrupted the continuity of classical and modern; a society and ultimately a culture torn from its origins cannot maintain itself, and inevitably declines into an arid plain. It is the task of the modern poet to salvage and reconstitute what he can of tradition. "The Waste Land" is in part an attempt to address the danger of a dying tradition, to palliate the effects so that the whole may survive.

What is missing from Romantic works for Eliot is a unified sense of literary history. Romanticism as an age is very different from earlier periods in that it attempted a sense of itself in relation to the past that was absolute. Romantics such as Shelley claimed authority over interpretation. They asserted their will not to be considered historically, to prove wrong statements like Eliot's "The difference between the present and the past is that the conscious present is an awareness of the past in a way and to an extent which the past's awareness of itself cannot show."[12] The Romantic writer, such as Rousseau, or Shelley, or Whitman, was aware of the self in a unique way, a way that always involved immediacy, not relativity. The nature of Romantic poetry is that it is organic, transcendent, regenerative: one's reading of a Romantic poem is in a sense always a first reading because it recreates itself in the experience. "Ode on a Grecian Urn" offers the physical form of ode and urn to history and time, but its meaning is outside of time and cannot be touched by earlier or subsequent theories. It asserts its pure identity in each reading. Subjective ideals cannot be incorporated into cultural history; the literary historian can only note a prevailing tendency, which leaves content untouched. Romantic content may be part of what Eliot refers to in the lines, "I have heard the key / turn in the door once and turn once only / We think of the key, each in his prison / Thinking of the key, each confirms a prison . . . ." Once locked into subjectivism, a society loses a sense of all but the immediate, ahistorical situation. In Eliot's theory of tradition, Romanticism leads to a cultural and spiritual dead end.

CHAPTER SIX: COLERIDGE IN "THE WASTE LAND"

The suggestion that "The Waste Land" contains allusions to Coleridge leads to two distinct critical repercussions. First, recognition of allusions to Coleridge and to Romanticism in general will affect our reading of Eliot's poem, as was discussed in the preceding chapter. The second issue arises from the reciprocal nature of a work of art and its tradition. In Eliot's critical system, a work of art's worth is judged by its relation to tradition; that very relation alters the ideal order of tradition. Thus "The Waste Land" as part of tradition changes our perception of other traditional works. The reader who knows Eliot's poem reads earlier poems in the context of a changed ideal order, for that is the concept's essence - art's organic coherence. When a critic today attempts to assess the work of Coleridge, that critic's assessment must take into account, even if indirectly, the effect of "The Waste Land" on the place of Coleridge in tradition. Coleridge's poems exist in relation to Eliot's in a general way through his theory of ideal order. The relation is then made more direct by Eliot's use of Coleridge in "The Waste Land" as a poet whose poems and theories threatened tradition, and whose work must be reassessed to distinguish its traditional elements from its destructive influence.

Reading Coleridge's poetry in the context of "The Waste Land" helps to illustrate how poems within the same tradition are organically related. By juxtaposing Coleridge's poems with "The Waste Land," one can identify Coleridge's traditional themes and images, and one can see the errors of his philosophical ideas as Eliot saw them. In Eliot's theory of tradition, each poem first stands on its own merits; its worth can also be assessed in relation to its author's criticism; finally, it connects both with those poems which preceded it in literary history and with those which came after. It is in this last context that the relationship of Coleridge's poems to Eliot's sense of the destruction of tradition appears. "The Waste Land" represents an age that has greater knowledge of the past than the past was able to have of itself, as Eliot observed in "Tradition and the Individual Talent." Reading Coleridge in light of Eliot clarifies that knowledge of what the particular works in literary history have meant for tradition.

In his study of poetic tradition Eliot paid particular attention to theme and imagery as measures of orthodoxy. That themes and images coincide in the poems of Coleridge and Eliot is by itself an irrelevant observation, for one could make the same comparison of nearly any two poets without claim to profundity. Eliot's poetic method of testing for traditional conformity forms the focus of critical interest here. His thematic test demonstrates the coherence of the allusions in "The Waste Land" within the poem and their representative nature in relation to the Western poetic tradition; one can judge the poems of Coleridge for traditional worth by considering their thematic content against the representative catalogue in "The Waste Land." The same method applies to the imagery incorporated in Coleridge's poems: how do his major images relate to traditonal use - how do they affect the "history" of each image?

In many cases, the thematic relationship between the poems of Coleridge and Eliot and the poems' common images show that their routes are similar but their destinations different. Three major poems of Coleridge - "The Rime of the Ancient Mariner," "Christabel," "Dejection: an Ode" - plus several minor ones, all relate thematically to "The Waste Land." "The Waste Land" and certain Coleridge poems depict similar conflicts, but their resolutions, and the feeling surrounding them, differ diametrically. The need for rebirth, a recreation of the spirit, evident especially in Coleridge's major poems, represents to Eliot a kind of historical authority, evidence that the need is universal in time and geography. Both poets use similar metaphorical female figures; Philomela is one specific coinciding symbol. The Christabel/Geraldine dichotomy of innocence and corruption finds several correlatives in "The Waste Land," with its dual symbols of nature and decay. The natural imagery ubiquitous in Coleridge is pared down for Eliot's purposes to a mountain/rock/water schema, and together with the image of spring diverges in symbolic meaning. In specific instances, the poet's voice echoes from poem to poem over the centuries, Coleridge's "music loud and long" worked out to its final empty and resigned statement of exhaustion in Eliot. Certain of his themes play off of Coleridge's and emphasize the loss, the glorious past and diminishing present of modern man, out of nature, out of art, the possessor of fragments and exhausted symbols.

The female personae in "The Waste Land" embody the themes of beauty and passion as regenerative forces, the intuitional or mystical powers of "vision" and the modern analogues of decay, corruption, sensual exhaustion, and chicanery. Procne's tragic murder of her children becomes Lil's abortion; Philomela's violent rape washes down to the typist's insensible passivity; Belladonna is in the service of an unseeing Madame Sosostris. The last two images, and the overall theme of beauty reverting to corruption, may be located in Coleridge's "The Nightingale," "Dejection: an Ode," and "Christabel."

In "The Nightingale," Coleridge quotes Milton's line from "Il Penseroso," "'Most musical, most melancholy' bird!" in order to "correct" a traditional association, reclaiming the nightingale as an image of natural joy.[1] In lines 34-39, Coleridge allies the view of the nightingale as a melancholy image with those out of nature:

> Youths and maidens most poetical
> Who lose the deepening twilights of the spring
> In ball rooms and hot theatres, they still
> Full of meek sympathy must heave their sighs
> O'er Philomela's pity-pleading strains.

Coleridge reclaims the bird from ancient associations and sentimental fancies as he rejects the interpretation formed in shallow, artificial society, divorced from natural truth. A quotation from Milton also begins Eliot's use of the Philomela/nightingale image in "A Game of Chess":

> Above the antique mantel was displayed
> As though a window gave upon the sylvan scene
> The change of Philomel, by the barbarous king
> So rudely forced; yet there the nightingale
> Filled all the desert with inviolable voice

The image in Eliot has an even more petrified context than that which Coleridge found so objectionable: the nightingale is seen in a picture above a mantel, viewed through the eyes of Satan, Philomela frozen like Mallarmé's swan in the constant conflict of beauty and destruction, the voice of nature obscured by bad art and modern corruption. The nightingale's "swift jug jug" in Coleridge's poem is a call to natural harmony; her cry in "The Waste Land" is a "jug jug to dirty ears." In "The Nightingale," Coleridge's quotation is an attempt to strip the image of the nightingale of its classical association with pain and melancholy, a poetic statement against tradition. His lines smother the living past and break the ties between Romantic and classical poetry, rendering the former, in Eliot's system, essentially meaningless and destructive to tradition. In "The Waste Land," Eliot's image of the nightingale corrects the Romantic influence by reinstating the classical background, in one direct way by using the Philomela/nightingale image in its original mythic connection.

In this instance, Eliot's poem is a rejection of Coleridge's image because for Eliot it is not enough to feel or to see; the poet must make sense of a perception in order to endow it with meaning for the reader. What poet and reader should share is not an emotion but a context for that emotion. The poet should interpret the significance and worth of experience instead of indulging in raw feeling. Given Eliot's context, Coleridge's use of the nightingale image is clearly too personal and denies the image's full resonance. Whatever particular association is intended in a poem, its force is greater if it rises from a multitude of meanings. Eliot's use of the nightingale retains the complexity of the image and enables the poem, and the reader, to combine the emotions and experience so that some new vision or knowledge is evinced. In the case of "The Waste Land," the history of the image is vital to its particular use in the poem; it illustrates themes of passion, pain, and loss, first in its mythological context, and then symbolically in the modern incapacity to react to the past and the spirit. The feminine nature of the image is lost in Coleridge's employment of it, which also renders it less evocative in Eliot's view. Coleridge creates a personal context for the image in his poem, which refers the reader to the poet rather than to traditional poetry. If one reads Eliot's lines with Coleridge's in mind, one gets a clear sense of how the loss of a cultural center comes about.

The Romantic era can once again be cited as the point of transformation from traditional values to selfish, unregenerative pursuits through the parallel themes and images in "Christabel" and "The Waste Land." Each poem opens with the topos of spring, shown in the first line of "The Waste Land," "April is the cruellest month," and lines 21-22 of "Christabel": "'Tis a month before the month of May / And the Spring comes slowly up this way." Unlike the traditional symbolic meaning of the topos, the connotations of renewed imagination in Coleridge introduce a new element of evil. The conflict in each poem is the choice between the good, regenerative life and the attraction to illusion and evil. For Coleridge, and in general for Romanticism in Europe and America, there is a kind of beauty in evil: it is seductive, an aesthetic idea rather than a moral issue, an alien yet strangely familiar part of the self. The demon in Coleridge's poetry is a compelling figure, horrible, perhaps, but appealing in a sensational way. The discovery of it in the self is startling, but also eerily refreshing, for it opens one to new visions and perceptions, and to the possibility of spiritual movement and growth. The Ancient Mariner owes his knowledge to his random act of evil, for example; in "The Aeolian Harp," a kind of thrill occurs from the speaker's brush with infidelity both to Sara and her God.

"Christabel" mirrors the divided nature of the female throughout "The Waste Land." Christabel and Geraldine embody innocence, passion, naiveté, and corruption. In Eliot's poem, the first two qualities are associated with women before the modern period; the last two are dominant in the waste land of the present. The female is a traditional symbol of beauty in its double nature of evil and ideal. The symbol of woman from Biblical days onward represents both corruption and fertility. It is interesting that when the figure appears in Coleridge's poems, he often leaves the poems as fragments: both "Christabel," with the figure of Geraldine, and "Kubla Khan," with the figure of the woman "wailing for her demon lover," are the most direct representations of the awful marriage of the two opposites.

Possibly the fragmentary form of these two Coleridge poems is an invitation to free play of the imagination, yet Coleridge intended to complete "Christabel" and claimed that it was only an interruption following his dream of Kubla Khan that prevented him from completing the poem. More likely he refrained from a literal statement of the implications of man's attraction to evil, something Eliot seemed to have recognized and condemned. Eliot's admiration for Baudelaire's poetry may in part come from Baudelaire's completed system of evil and knowledge. In "Une Charogne" especially, one can see how the poet works through the beautiful companion's relationship to a decaying carcass:

--Et pourtant vous serez semblable à cette ordure,
 À cette horrible infection,
Étoile de mes yeux, soleil de ma nature,
 Vous, mon ange et ma passion!

Oui! telle vous serez, Ô la reine des grâces,
 Après les derniers sacrements,

> Quand vous irez sous l'herbe et les floraisons grasses,
>
> Moisir parmi les ossements.
>
> Alors, ô ma beauté, dites à la vermine
>
> Qui vous mangera de baisers,
>
> Que j'ai gardé la forme et l'essence divine
>
> De mes amours décomposés![2]

Baudelaire's imagery unites the ideal form and decadent matter. Evil as a regenerative force is not extolled but accepted as a painful truth, both poetically and spiritually. Coleridge's aesthetic resists the knowledge; Eliot's poem suggests that such resistance ends in aesthetic and moral failure.

In "Christabel," good, in the form of the departed mother, is wrapped in a shroud, the garment of decay. The "mastiff bitch," also a female figure, alone reacts to the presence of evil around her, howling softly because she "sees my lady's shroud," making an "angry moan" when Geraldine passes by. Evil is cloaked in beauty and commands the attention of all around. The innocence of Christabel is at the center of the struggle; her nature is not yet clarified as she is drawn by both forces, imitating Geraldine's serpent eyes and baleful look at one point, then regaining her guileless mien. The image of evil suggests, seduces, and inspires. It recreates old Sir Leoline's courtly nature. It brings dreams and awareness to Christabel. Whatever the specific effects, its general nature seems to be valuable to the poet. No Miltonic notion of the "fortunate fall" lies behind the imagery, but a purely Romantic notion of sensual release, limitless knowledge, and amoral experience.

In "The Waste Land," symbols of good and evil are juxtaposed as in

Coleridge's poem, with the difference that the union of good and evil is impossible, unlike the Geraldine figure. Eliot's poem offers a choice, not a dialectic. Evil by itself breeds evil if no external force enters to purify it. A "burnished throne" is an entirely insulated symbol of the artistically living past despite its present inhabitant, a modern and thus spiritually decaying woman who suffers from bad nerves. The spiritual connection of Christabel and her departed mother is assailed by the evil Geraldine, who succeeds in overcoming the maternal power and in insinuating herself into Christabel's family concerns. But "The Waste Land" contradicts the Romantic convention of good and evil commingling in a creative bond. Eliot's poem suggests that evil, the sign of a loss of a clear guiding spirit, degrades and corrupts across time: "O the moon shone bright on Mrs. Porter / And on her daughter / They wash their feet in soda water . . . ." The moral corruption of the mother, Sweeney's prostitute, is the accepted legacy of the daughter. The parallel of these images to the images in Coleridge's poem illustrates an aspect of the breakdown of poetic tradition through the loss of objectively determined standards. The corruption of the poetic process by theories of subjectivism must lead to a loss of cultural unity, a split between life and art with the ensuing denaturalization and demeaning of both. Eliot's female figures counter Coleridge's symbols of the imagination. Not creativity but destruction comes from the conflict of the individual with his tradition.

A female image in "Dejection: an Ode" concerns the cycle of natural life and symbolizes spiritual regeneration as well. The old Moon pales in the lap of the new, a herald of storm that arouses the soul. The image seems directly related to Coleridge's theory of poetic creation. In the context of Eliot's poem, the connection of feminine and natural imagery has undergone a fundamental change. Regeneration and inspiration come at a price: the acceptance of temporal death by belief in objective, external values. The self cannot recreate itself; the Romantic process is a delusion. One cannot impose a subjective view of nature and expect that eternal value will reside in it. Eliot does not idealize the "rain and squally blast." For him, the image is filled with pain, sacrifice, and passion, in the root sense of the word.

The female imagery in Coleridge's poem once again unites the fresh, full, fertile side of a feminine entity with its antithesis, the old, limp, and faded precursor. The new beauty replaces the outworn, eclipsing the old dimness with her shining power. It is a cyclical process in which the new embraces the old, gaining much of her value through the contrasting states of exhaustion and abundance. The physical reality of the image joins the two sides of the single entity: a shiny crescent, extending until it disappears in darkness at each end, seems to embrace an empty darkness, a form without content. One can trace the old Moon's figure, but its center had faded, its brilliance decayed. The joining of the opposites ensures continued regeneration; the image signals rain, which "might startle this dull pain, and make it move and live."

Eliot's images of decay, on the other hand, emphasize the possibility that the individual may be incapable of renewal. To rely on the individual's power is to invite extinction. Without tradition, a poet will be unable to produce works of value; without objective standards, man will be unable to recognize value. The source of renewal must be impersonal and universal. Coleridge's evocation of the mood of dejection is an adequate summary of the tone of a waste land in its physical and spiritual setting: "A grief without a pang, void, dark, and drear / A stifled, drowsy, unimpassioned grief / Which finds no natural outlet, no relief." The spiritual loss in Eliot's poem is generalized onto the symbolic landscape: "And the dead tree gives no shelter, the cricket no relief." The "grief without a pang" echoes in the "dying with a little patience." Many of Eliot's images are "void, dark, and drear": the "dead land," "stony rubbish," "brown fog of a winter dawn," "dead sound," and "cracked earth." The unimpassioned figures in "The Waste Land" suffer, but silently, passively, without hope for or effort toward regeneration. The relief of natural outlets - emotions, sexual unions - is no longer possible because man cannot make a commitment, the "awful daring of a moment's surrender." Coleridge claims an internal creative force; Eliot insists on the subjugation of the self to a greater force outside. One needs to escape subjectivity if one is to find relief. The course of modern life is away from nature and challenges the sense of individual identity and stability. Romanticism does not offer a means to continued existence because it rejects a compromise with historical reality. To paraphrase Eliot, we are the past, we are its result. Poets who create poetry from personal emotion condemn the future to repetition of those emotions and block access to earlier experience. The emotions lose their historical context and burn themselves out. The dying figures in "The Waste Land" result from their Romantic past.

Two specific lines in "The Waste Land" recall "Kubla Khan" to mind. Given Eliot's sense of the English poetic tradition, both Coleridge and "Kubla Khan" are likely standards of Romantic poets and poems. The creative vigor of the latter poem is especially pronounced and outshines all of Coleridge's other poems in its energy: it vibrates with uncurbed drives, wild power, and defiant exaltation of poetic force in the face of eighteenth-century poetic theory and general social misapprobation. The speaker claims metaphoric descent from an Eastern ruler in an exotic realm; like Kubla Khan, he faces traditional voices crying out against his art. He asserts his cause and devotes himself to creating natural wonders and miraculous works, all for his own delight. The Alph, unlike Eliot's sacred rivers, is holy as the source of poetic inspiration and is a symbol of the internal creative stream; it is not an historical and spiritual entity like the Ganges or Thames. From Kubla Khan's river springs the enclosed land of pleasure (i.e. the poem itself) defined by "walls and towers" (i.e. the metaphorical structure of the poem). The speaker vows to recreate the vision, or "with music loud and long / I would build that dome in air." Eliot adapted these lines to the content of his poem, using part of them verbatim to achieve the effect of including the Romantic aesthetic, represented by Coleridge, in the historical structure of the poem and thus implying the responsibility of Romanticism for the birth of the modern waste land.

The middle part of the section "What the Thunder Said" symbolizes a descent into hell; it is evoked through images in earlier lines that mimic the delirium preceding a death by dehydration. The lines "If there were water / And no rock / If there were rock / And also water / And water / A spring . . ." are desperate, dying words of crazed despair, an irrational fantasy ending in the horrible but again rational realization, "But there is no water." The next experience is a series of dream-like, inexplicable visions showing the loss of rational faculties and an inability any longer to make sense of sensual data:

Who is the third who walks always beside you?
When I count, there are only you and I together
But when I look ahead up the white road
There is always another one walking beside you

> Gliding wrapt in a brown mantle, hooded
> I do not know whether a man or a woman
> -But who is that on the other side of you?
>
> What is that sound high in the air
> Murmur of maternal lamentation
> Who are those hooded hordes swarming
> Over endless plains, stumbling in cracked earth
> Ringed by the flat horizon only
> What is the city over the mountains
> Cracks and reforms and bursts in the violet air
> Falling towers

Then the speaker re-emerges in hell, where "music" is fiddled on a woman's "long, black hair" and "bats with baby faces" "crawled head downward down a blackened wall," an awful joining of apparent innocence and ugly nature. What he sees is that "upside down in air were towers / Tolling reminiscent bells, that kept the hours / And voices singing out of empty cisterns and exhausted wells." The lines evoke Dante on one level; they also seem to be a tour through Coleridge's Romantic imagery and the cultural effect of Romantic poetry.

Some of the imagery in those lines comes directly from "Kubla Khan." "Towers" are the Romantic poems, just as Coleridge referred to his particular work, and they are created "in air," as the speaker of "Kubla Khan" proclaims, that is, free from traditional, outdated literary precepts, and sprung from the poet's imagination. They presume to toll the death knell of tradition, the earlier works that for Eliot were the organizing principles of Western culture in their role as measures of progress in cultural coherence. Eliot counters the joyous claim of the Romantic poet; in reality, he is one of the "voices singing out of empty cisterns and exhausted wells." The Romantic vision of the sacred spring is a death-dream, a delusion produced by spiritual aridity. Romanticism is a path to hell, for it is a deregulation of values. "Upside down in air were towers . . ."; the vocabulary is Coleridge's, and Eliot very likely intended us to hear the echo and incorporate it into his poetic structure.

Earlier, in "The Fire Sermon," Eliot incorporates a phrase from "Kubla Khan" in the line "Sweet Thames, run softly till I end my song / Sweet Thames, run softly, for I speak not loud or long." Coleridge's speaker exclaims that "with music loud and long" he will create his poem. Eliot's speaker utters the word "song" with an ironic effect, however, for his words are not musical, but become a chanted lament, spoken, not sung, in a quiet, un-energetic fashion. A line from Marvell's "To His Coy Mistress" follows, but it reminds the poet of the decay of present time instead of the celebration of life it once defended. The direct allusion to "Kubla Khan" and the negation of the energy with which it was originally uttered force the reader to "read" both poems at once. Eliot's allusion juxtaposes Thames and Alph; Renaissance, Romantic, and modern; classical and waste. The modern poet has no belief to celebrate, no sense of self worth extolling. His art has turned away from unified conceptions of the world and intimations of divine connections. The poetic material available to him is urban corruption, historical discontinuity, and leveled emotions. By evoking Coleridge's line, the consequences of asserting ego over tradition are illuminated.

The use of exoticisms is a signature of much Romantic literature, from

Hoffmann, to Byron, to Hugo. In Coleridge's work, the narrative poems have many images and references to the East as a land of strange splendor. Geraldine in "Christabel" has the beauty of a "lady of a far countree." Kubla Khan is the ruler of a mythic Eastern land. The image usually serves to make of the alien its own material. The very strangeness of the East has sublime appeal for the Romantic; its unfamiliarity stimulates the poetic process. The worth of exoticism lies in its very unconnectedness to Western tradition, provoking an escape from classical modes in particular. The "East" is other, and hence does not partake of Western morality or aesthetics. "There you feel free," there you may imagine a reality apart.

In "The Waste Land," the East also looms as an alien land whose image has great allure for the poet. Its allure in this case, however, lies in its mythical and religious roots, not some mistily splendorous picture of domes or dark ladies. In contrast to Romantic use of the image, Eliot's is historical and implies traditional associations. Buddhist parables, sacred rivers, and native language document a living tradition known to the Western poet in a scholarly way only. Eliot ends his poem with references to Indian culture as a contrast and warning to the West. Unlike our own culture, which lies in fragments heaped together instead of in ideal order, the Buddhist and Hindu tradition maintains its ancient sources in the present. The Ganges is a living spiritual symbol, in contrast to the Thames, a desecrated and deserted receptacle for refuse and bad confessions. Our myths are forgotten or become accusatory by reminding us of past passion and sacrifice. Modern man lives the "Fire Sermon" without understanding its message, for no Augustine remains to interpret the "cauldron of unholy loves" singing all about his ears. The end of the poem is a breakdown of the West, an appeal to the East: we have lost our cultural foundation and in desperation seek out some other structure for support.

A minor Coleridge poem, "The Pains of Sleep," has thematic relevance to "The Waste Land" in its presentation of the conflict between moral and social order and the darker human impulse that bring about alienation and degradation. The consciousness of the speaker in Coleridge's poem includes the external natural world but also the world of night, of wild dreams and uncensored imagination. He confronts the power of his unharnessed will to desire evil and dispense with shame, to indulge in excessive passion with full awareness of his other, social self. The knowledge stuns at first, then disgusts, and ultimately leads to repentance - tears of suffering - and a will to be regenerated - a search for love. The metaphors present the poetic process as a dream become a nightmare through the social and moral resistance of the poet's external reality. The moral order disappears in the imaginative process, for the poet transcends its constrictions, yet must return to them, guilty and contrite. That struggle is used in turn by Eliot to signify not the poetic process but the price of subjectivity: chaos in the individual and hence in his culture. Eliot's poem affects the poem of the past: read in the context of Eliot's sense of tradition, the conflict of the poem becomes a symbol of the conflict of Romanticism with tradition. It is Romantic theory used against itself.

The speaker in Coleridge's poem wakes "in agony" from a nightmare vision: "A lurid light, a trampling throng / Sense of intolerable wrong . . . ." The overwhelming environment of evil oppresses the speaker through the uncertainty of its source: it seems alien, yet is within. Unrecognizable shapes appear in disfiguring, exaggerating light, a sick perception that brings horror into the soul, for the shapes, though unrecognized, are still extensions of the self. At several points in "The Waste Land," the speaker looks out on his surroundings, the city, and finds equally alienating figures that are yet part of him in some structure greater than the individual and encompassing him. First Madame Sosostris "reads" the situation: "I see crowds of people, walking round in a ring." Then the speaker looks over the city: "A crowd flowed over London Bridge, so many." In the final section, the nightmare sequence, as the speaker approaches the final confrontation, he too has visions of a grotesque throng of unrecognized shapes: "Who are those hooded hordes swarming / Over endless plains . . . ." The same poetic conflict of Coleridge's poem is transposed to the cultural and spiritual conflict of modern Western culture. Instead of an aesthetic issue, however, Eliot makes it clear in his Notes that his line refers to an historical basis: the "decay of Eastern Europe." The speaker has too limited a consciousness and too outworn a symbology to make sense of the chaos he sees within and without. The tone is one of fear, pain, "intolerable wrong." In Coleridge's poem, the speaker struggles helplessly: "Thirst of revenge, the powerless will / Still baffled, and yet burning still!" Thirst and debilitated will are common images throughout much of Coleridge's poetry and "The Waste Land," in the one case used to describe the Romantic poet's condition, in the second, man's, partly because of his Romantic heritage, I suggest. The Romantic poet reacts against an overly restrictive tradition and too vigilant society. His antithesis is reached in the figure in "The Waste Land," in whose world things fall apart through the loss of tradition and the inability to connect individual, society, religion, and art.

Line 27 of "Pains of Sleep" illustrates the similarity in feeling but difference in source of the anguish felt by both the Romantic poet and the modern speaker:

"Desire with loathing strangely mixed . . . ." Like Eliot's image of April "mixing / Memory and desire," the line expresses a conflict between a natural drive and an opposing inner force. Each speaker feels an instinctive desire to create, to revive from dullness. In the poems, loathing and memory are the equivalents which work against the impulse to be reborn. The memory of the speaker in the waste land is of a life of pain and sacrifice; in the modern confusion of values, "a little life" is preferable to a difficult process of life, death, and regeneration. By remaining insulated, the speaker may dispense with feeling and find protection under the cover of winter's suspension of life. But the desire for spring enters his consciousness through the natural order represented by April. From outside the dormant individual comes a force that impels him to the necessary process. The desire and loathing in Coleridge's poem come from within and then are externalized: "For all seemed guilt, remorse, or woe / My own or others still the same / Life-stifling fear, soul-stifling shame." The conflict in the poet's unconscious distorts his perceptions and leads him to impose his personal feelings on the world outside himself and to adopt the standards of that outside world, applying them inappropriately to his artistic process. In each poem, the self is a prison and the creative imperative is met with confusion and fear; life and spirit are stifled.

In the extended context of "The Waste Land," Eliot's criticism, and the traditional works which he evokes most often throughout his writings, the most common theme is the relationship of the individual to a universal system of good and evil. Just as Eliot focused on Dante, Shakespeare, and Baudelaire in many of his essays and relied on their works for many of his images, one might consider Coleridge's "The Rime of the Ancient Mariner" to be the Romantic poem most acceptable and most amenable to his theory of tradition. A reading of the Coleridge poem within the context of "The Waste Land" demonstrates the traditional ties between the poems in terms of theme and imagery. In this new context, Coleridge's poem can be considered beyond the limits of Romanticism; one can place it within the ordered system of tradition to evaluate what Eliot might have judged to be its universal aspect.

The theme of suffering as prelude to rebirth is sounded throughout "The Waste Land." Man must undergo a process of expiation for his sin and guilt, either on an individual level or through the mediation of a scapegoat figure. As has been widely noted, this last image is common to the pagan culture as Eliot perceived it through Jessie Weston's work. Both in vegetation myths and Christian theology, water images are prevalent. Eliot also used water as one dominant image and associated the suffering individual or scapegoat with it. The "drowned Phoenician sailor" is a recurring and thematically binding figure in the poem, as Eliot indicates in his Notes. This image and its related theme of death and rebirth by water suggests a tie between "The Waste Land" and Coleridge in "The Ancient Mariner." Some of the images in Eliot's poem have thematic correlation to those found in "The Ancient Mariner," as a single reading of both poems reveals. Eliot's affinity for works that integrate religious experience and common existence is pronounced, and of all Coleridge's poems, "The Ancient Mariner" should be the most acceptable and meaningful within his system of judgment. In each poem the general theme and subject is man's path from innocence to evil and then through suffering to spriritual regeneration. In each case a seafarer is a central symbol of the common man, open to sinful urges, able to stand as a kind of "cross-bearer," and on his way to final redemption. The mariner, and his analogue the fisherman, are fixed figures across the centuries from ancient Phoenicia to modern London. Their appearance at various points in "The Waste Land" combines several major themes of the poem.

Lines 31-42 enclose the incident with the hyacinth girl with references to Tristan and Isolde, specifically to the scene in which Tristan looks to the sea for the ship bearing the life-saving Isolde. But the ship does not appear: "Oed und leer das Meer." No guiding mariner is in evidence; only the instinctive hope of the sufferer directs his eyes to the water that signifies salvation. But without faith or spiritual commitment, the sufferer finds no relief. In line 47, the "drowned Phoenician sailor" appears in the Tarot reading. He is the questioner's card, the significator, the symbol of the individual seeker. His physical depiction comes in part from Shakespeare's Tempest: "Those are pearls that were his eyes." In the "Ancient Mariner," the Wedding Guest "is spellbound by the eye of the old seafaring man," in Coleridge's note; the line in the poem is "He holds him with his glittering eye," and throughout the poem he carries the epithet "the bright-eyed Mariner." The eye in Coleridge's poem signifies the greater vision of the Mariner who sees within and without a natural moral imperative. But the opaqueness of the pearly eye in Eliot's poem is not a symbol of vision; the blind Tiresias performs the function of seer and finds no such moral order. The pearl is more a symbol of the value of suffering, a second sight after death, as suffering transforms individual perception to vision of the absolute. The symbol seems connected to the preceding hyacinth garden sequence: "Looking into the heart of light, the silence." The vocabulary is that of a mystical experience. The sheen of the pearl is at once illuminating but not clarifying. Its sensual properties are contradictory: light and opacity, beauty from decay. Later in the poem, Phlebas the Phoenician reappears, having "forgot the cry of gulls," and he is held up to the living as a picture of their fate. He was once "handsome and tall."

Throughout the imagery the purely sensual is what dies; no vision, hearing, or tactile awareness remains after drowning, but pearls come from the change of life to death. Whether the eyes of the sailor, as in "The Waste Land," or eyes of the king, as in the Tempest, the true worth of vision is not sensual, as it is for Romanticism in general, but spiritual, and can be attained only through great sacrifice. Even Coleridge's Mariner has vision only after suffering "like one that hath been seven days drowned." The modern, and thus fraudulent, seer, however, advises the seeker to "fear death by water," thus discouraging him from the necessary sacrifice.

Eliot connects the ancient and modern mariner again in line 70, when the speaker accosts "Stetson" as a comrade from the sea battle at Mylae. There is a kind of re-enactment of the questioning in the Madame Sosostris section when the seeker, using a line from the Inferno, stops him to ask about a corpse blooming. The pagan and Christian imagery in this section underlines the modern fear of and alienation from the cycle of death and rebirth. Webster's dog has changed from foe to friend; the modern man hopes for an undisturbed grave much as he resents the reviving spirit of cruel April. Coleridge's mariner parallels Eliot's sailor as the symbol of necessary suffering. Baudelaire's famous line closes the first part of "The Waste Land," an allusion to the whole of Les Fleurs du mal which connects several strands of Eliot's poem at this point. First, Eliot seems to be presenting a theme very close to that of Baudelaire: both refer to a similar system of decay and regeneration. Both poets use the image of the modern city as hell. Both use religious imagery and vocabulary. They share an unromantic belief in order outside the self. And related to the present discussion is Baudelaire's poem, "L'Albatros," which Eliot may have intended as a tertiary echo from his poem to Coleridge's to Baudelaire's. Baudelaire's albatross is a scapegoat for the mariners, much as the mariner bearing the albatross is in Coleridge's poem. Eliot's Phlebas is a symbol for the rest of mankind. The historical context of the image and its use in Eliot's poem unite several synbols into one, to illuminate the continuity of ancient and modern, and to include the valid, because traditional, essence of Coleridge's poem.

The inescapable images in both "The Ancient Mariner" and "The Waste Land" are water, thirst, and deliverance, with a setting of a fertility scene or marriage and the use of bird symbolism. Coleridge's mariner survives the polar storm and empty drift in an icy sea; the albatross then appears like a messenger from God and the crew is delivered: "The ice did split with a thunder fit / The helmsman steered us through!" The same salvation imagery appears in "What the Thunder Said," although it is used as a token of hope, not its realization. The thunder speaks in Eliot's poem to signify the possibility of finding deliverance from the waste land. The "correct" answer, "Dayadhvam," is the same as that at which the Ancient Mariner arrives: sympathize. A recognition of supreme godly force is imperative in each instance. For Eliot's speaker, the recognition is cautious but yearning: "The boat responded / Gaily, to the hand expert with sail and oar / The sea was calm, your heart would have responded / Gaily, when invited, beating obedient / To controlling hands." What comes as natural feeling in Coleridge is a fearful response in Eliot, so alienated is the waste land inhabitant to sympathetic reaction. The helmsman in Eliot's poem is an unknown figure, recognized for his power and his role as possible savior, but there is still fear and hesitation in the heart.

Frost and heat in each poem signify the stages of suffering and the need for expiation. The Mariner is first trapped in ice and mist. Eliot's city dweller travels "under the brown fog of a winter dawn." The frost prevents him from moving, as it did Jesus' followers in the "frosty silence in the gardens." Frost indicates a moribund state of the soul, when there is no will to hope. It occurs again in the section drawn from both Shackleton's Antarctic expedition and Christ's journey to Emmaus, where the traveler cannot recognize the guiding figure. The route to deliverance is an agonizing process of purification through fire, suggested by the allusion to Arnaut Daniel in the Purgatorio. The Ancient Mariner witnesses the unnatural transformation of the sea into a rotten, burning field populated by "slimy things." In each poem, thirst is the punishment: "And every tongue, through utter drought / Was withered at the root," in Coleridge; "Here is no water but only rock / Rock and no water and the sandy road," in Eliot. The two images of frost and heat meet in Coleridge's line, " Moon beams bemocked the sultry main / Like April hoar-frost spread." The sufferers in each poem dream of water in their delirium: the waste land sufferer hears the "dripdrop"; the Mariner is surrounded by water that seems to burn: he looks at the ship buckets and "dreamt that they were filled with dew."

The figure of the Mariner with the albatross hung about his neck is the scapegoat for his and his companions' guilt. The hanged man from the Tarot pack is Eliot's symbol of the necessary sufferer, and in his Notes to the poem he connects him to the hooded figure in the journey to Emmaus section. Even after his freedom from the burden takes place, the Ancient Mariner must carry on his role as a spiritual exemplum by telling his tale to those who are most in need of hearing it. His is not only an individual experience of guilt and redemption but has symbolic relevance to all. The subjective experience is generalized to a universal end.

The Romantic aspect of this poem in its theme of natural goodness does not transgress Eliot's notion of commitment to an organizing system of belief. The mariner is the same symbol of the necessary spiritual path as is the drowned sailor, hanged god, or Jesus Christ. The symbol of water associated with all four figures signifies their, and thus man's, transformation from the arid human plain to spiritual life through suffering and self-sacrifice. The Mariner's unconscious blessing of the water-snakes, an act free of selfish concern and offered up despite his personal state of pain and despair, brings on the life-saving rain and washes away the symbol of his guilt. The sacrifice of the god/king in pagan vegetation rituals brings on the spring rain and renewal. Jesus' baptism as man provides the saving example of Christian religion, and his death redeems hope for spiritual immortality. The death by water of Phlebas is each man's lot and only route to salvation: Phlebas "entering the whirlpool" passes from the material world into another realm; the Ancient Mariner watches as "upon the whirl, where sank the ship / The boat spun round and round." Water reclaims the bodies and releases the souls in each case.

Coleridge's image of "Life-in-Death" is akin to the image of Phlebas and to the female imagery throughout "The Waste Land." Eliot presents image after image of the cycle of death and rebirth, from the opening of the poem set in springtime, the change of seasons, and the "handful of dust" in "Burial of the Dead," through the Christ imagery and thunder and rain of the final section, where man is in the last stage of spiritual corruption and his choice must be made between renewed life or ultimate exhaustion. Eliot's poem reverses Coleridge's image ot death-in-life, a description of modern man's spiritual and cultural state: "A crowd flowed over London Bridge, so many / I had not thought death had undone so many"; man is "dying / with a little patience." Coleridge's Mariner is the prize in Death and Life-in-Death's dice game; he belongs to the latter's realm of those who walk with transcendent knowledge, wandering teachers of man's fate. The Mariner must forever perform the "penance of life": "Since then, at an uncertain hour / That agony returns / And till my ghastly tale is told / This heart within me burns." A recognition of a force beyond the individual, perhaps God, perhaps tradition, is central to the tension of each poem. Each points to a belief that will survive the individual's death and which thus provides a kind of immortality. The natural moral world predominates in "The Ancient Mariner"; a living cultural tradition, one that combines art and religion, is at stake in "The Waste Land."

Eliot's poem redirects one's reading of Coleridge's so that the saving elements are emphasized, which perhaps represents Eliot's effort to assimilate part of Romanticism into an ordered sense of Western culture. When "The Ancient Mariner" is read in Eliot's context, the reader's perception of Coleridge's poem is accompanied by a sense of value and danger. In The Waste Land in Different Voices, A.D. Moody discussed the parallel between Eliot's and Coleridge's poems:

> The correspondence with "Ancient Mariner" is revealing. The mariner too

sees all about him a universe of death, as the expression or consequence of deadened imagination . . . The mariner had seen as loathsome what he now can bless; it is in and through his perceptions and rhythmical expression of them that the great change occurs from death to life. In "The Waste Land" to sympathize with instead of coldly judging the Thames-daughters . . . is to begin to break out of the prison of the alienated self . . . .[3]

"The Ancient Mariner" becomes a traditional poem according to Eliot's criteria by incorporating the theme of spiritual renewal through self-sacrifice. It can be allied with the same theme in earlier works in the Western tradition; it conforms in an individual way. "The Waste Land" strengthens the traditional basis for the poetic concern with renewal, and helps to clarify the place of Coleridge's work within the ideal order of tradition.

That "the past should be altered by the present as much as the present is directed by the past" is the fundamental theory in Eliot's critical system that provides a logical means for the integration of Romanticism in Western tradition.[4] In "The Waste Land," he addressed the disorder represented by Romantic aesthetics. Just as history confines Romanticism to a specific literary period, Eliot, through his poem, confines it to a phase in the changing ideal order of Western literature. Romantic aesthetics becomes part of history, not tradition; only those themes, images, and poetic theories from past ages that were reworked by various Romantic artists enter the tradition, and those themes, images, and theories are in turn reworked by artists of later ages. What remains is not Romanticism, but Eliot's isolation of the universal elements of it. Eliot was able to reject Romanticism in literary history, on the level of individual poems and as a literary period; he rejected all that the term "Romantic" came to symbolize in his thought: the adolescent, the fragmentary, the subjective approach to art. He treated those aspects of Romanticism as extra-literary and so untraditional and unimportant.

Just as "The Waste Land" provides a context for some Romantic poetry, Eliot's essays form a context for Romantic critical and poetic theory. His works emphasize the traditional ideas of Coleridge, Wordsworth, Goethe, and Poe especially, to draw their universal ideas into tradition while excluding their Romantic context. The idea of the poet-critic justifies such selectivity. Since Eliot promoted a belief in the equivalence of poetic and critical ideas, one need not rely on a writer's poetry as a basis for assessing that writer's worth in tradition. The line of poet-critics like Dryden, Johnson, and Coleridge was one that Eliot could view with a sense of continuity, and one to which we may append his name as a poet-critic whose poetry and criticism served the same end of shaping out of the diverse material of literary history a coherent sense of literary values.

Notes to Chapter One

[1] Frank Kermode, Romantic Image (London: Routledge and Kegan Paul, 1957), p. 43.

[2] See C.K. Stead, The New Poetic (London: Hutchinson University Library, 1964).

[3] See Edward Lobb, T.S. Eliot and the Romantic Critical Tradition (London: Routledge and Kegan Paul, 1981).

[4] See Eloise Knapp Hay, T.S. Eliot's Negative Way (Cambridge, Ma.: Harvard University Press, 1982).

[5] George Bornstein, Transformations of Romanticism in Yeats, Eliot, and Stevens (Chicago: University of Chicago Press, 1976), p. 95.

[6] Ibid. p. 95.

[7] Ibid. p. xii.

[8] Ibid. p. 23.

[9] Austin Warren and Rene Wellek, Theory of Literature (New York: Harcourt, Brace and World, Inc., 1970.), p. 266.

[10] Bornstein, p. 19.

[11] Ibid. p. 121.

[12] "Wordsworth and Coleridge," in The Use of Poetry and the Use of Criticism, 2nd ed. (1964; rpt. London: Faber and Faber Ltd., 1968), pp. 68-69; see also "Shelley and Keats," p. 99 (hereafter cited as The Use of Poetry).

[13] "The Modern Mind," in The Use of Poetry, pp. 128-29.

[14] Victor Brombert, "T.S. Eliot and the Romantic Heresy," Yale French

Studies, No. 13 (1965), pp. 3-16.

¹⁵ "Introduction," The Use of Poetry, p. 33.

¹⁶ Bornstein, p. 97.

¹⁷ "Byron," in On Poetry and Poets (1943; rpt. New York: The Noonday Press, 1970), pp. 223-24.

¹⁸ "Byron," p. 226.

¹⁹ Ibid., p. 239.

²⁰ Ibid., p. 234.

²¹ Ibid., p. 232.

²² See "Swinburne as Poet," in The Sacred Wood (1920; rpt. London: Methuen & Co. Ltd., 1964), p. 147.

²³ "Shelley and Keats," in The Use of Poetry, p. 96.

²⁴ Ibid., p. 89.

²⁵ "The Music of Poetry," in Selected Prose of T.S. Eliot, ed. Frank Kermode (New York: Harcourt Brace Jovanovich and Farrar, Straus and Giroux, 1975), pp. 108-09 (hereafter cited as Selected Prose).

²⁶ Grover Smith, T.S. Eliot's Poetry and Plays (Chicago: University of Chicago Press, 1950), p. 3.

²⁷ "What Is a Classic?" in Selected Prose, p. 122.

²⁸ John D. Margolis, T.S. Eliot's Intellectual Development (Chicago: University of Chicago Press, 1972), p. 8.

²⁹ Irving Babbitt, Rousseau and Romanticism (New York: Houghton Mifflin Co., 1919), p. 38; p. 145.

³⁰ Margolis, pp. 10-11.

³¹ Babbitt, p. 391.

32 F.H. Bradley, Appearance and Reality, 2nd ed. (1893; London: George Allen Unwin Ltd., 1897), p. 22.

33 Ibid., p. 549.

34 Ibid., p. 525.

35 "Yeats," in Selected Prose, p. 248.

Notes to Chapter Two

1 "Hamlet," in Selected Prose, p. 49.

2 "Baudelaire," in Selected Essays (New York: Harcourt, Brace and World, Inc., 1960), p. 374.

3 Lewis Freed, T.S. Eliot: Aesthetics and History (La Salle, Il.: Open Court, 1962), p. 90.

4 "Hamlet," p. 49.

5 "Andrew Marvell," in Selected Essays, p. 251.

6 Ibid., p. 255.

7 Barbara Everett, "Eliot's Marianne: 'The Waste Land' and Its Poetry of Europe," Review of English Studies, No. 31 (1980), p. 51.

8 Smith, p. 3.

9 from Madame Bovary (Paris: Editions Gallimard et Librairie Générale Française, 1961), p. 146.

10 "'Ulysses', Order, and Myth," in Selected Prose, p. 177.

11 "Baudelaire," pp. 378-79.

12 "Introduction, The Sacred Wood, p. xii.

13 Ibid.

[14] Irving Babbitt, The Masters of Modern French Criticism (1912; rpt. New York: The Noonday Press, 1963), p. 66.

[15] Ibid., p. 2.

[16] "Baudelaire," p. 375.

[17] "The Function of Criticism," in Selected Essays, p. 15.

[18] "The Development of Leibniz's Monadism," Monist, 26, No. 4 (Oct. 1916), p. 556.

[19] Bradley, p. 322.

[20] Freed, pp. 84-85.

[21] "Blake," in The Sacred Wood, pp. 157-58.

[22] "Leibniz's Monads and Bradley's Finite Centres," Monist, p. 566.

[23] "The Metaphysical Poets," in Selected Essays, p. 248.

[24] "Reflections on 'Vers Libre'," in Selected Prose, p. 35.

[25] "The Possibility of a Poetic Drama," in The Sacred Wood, p. 66.

[26] Noted in Robert L. Beare, "T.S. Eliot and Goethe," Germanic Review, 28 (Dec. 1953), p. 244.

[27] "Goethe as the Sage," in On Poetry and Poets, p. 243.

[28] "Baudelaire," pp. 371-72.

[29] Sean Lucy, T.S. Eliot and Idea of Tradition (New York: Barnes and Noble, Inc., 1960), p. 70.

[30] "Review: Israfel," Nation and Athenaeum, 41, No. 7 (21 May 1927), p. 219.

[31] "Imperfect Critics," in The Sacred Wood, p. 31.

[32] "Andrew Marvell," in Selected Essays, pp. 259-60.

[33] "The Possibility of a Poetic Drama," p. 62.

[34] Margolis, pp. 10-11.

[35] "Dante," in The Sacred Wood, p. 162.

[36] "Tradition and the Individual Talent," in The Sacred Wood, p. 55.

[37] "Shelley and Keats," in The Use of Poetry, pp. 98-99.

[38] Note to Section II, "Dante," in Selected Essays, p. 231.

[39] "Wordsworth and Coleridge," in The Use of Poetry, p. 77.

[40] F.O. Matthiessen, The Achievement of T.S. Eliot (New York: Oxford University Press, 1959), p. 144.

[41] "Goethe as the Sage," in On Poetry and Poets," p. 254.

[42] "Dante," in Selected Essays, pp. 232-33.

[43] "Baudelaire," in Selected Essays, p. 379.

[44] Bradley, p. 3.

[45] Complete Plays of T.S. Eliot (New York: Harcourt, Brace & World Inc., 1967), p. 179.

[46] Ibid., p. 188.

[47] "Blake," in The Sacred Wood, p. 158.

[48] "Wordsworth and Coleridge," in The Use of Poetry, p. 67.

[49] Ethel F. Cornwell, The Still Point (New Brunswick: Rutgers University Press, 1962), p. 74.

[50] "What Is a Classic?" in Selected Prose, p. 126.

[51] Ibid., p. 119.

[52] "The Function of Criticism," in Selected Essays, pp. 12-13.

[53] "Imperfect Critics," in The Sacred Wood, p. 5.

Notes to Chapter Three

1 "The Perfect Critic," in The Sacred Wood, p.5.

2 Ibid. p. 14.

3 Ibid. p. 12.

4 Ibid. pp. 14-15.

5 "Imperfect Critics," in The Sacred Wood, p. 24.

6 "The Perfect Critic," p. 15.

7 Introduction to The Use of Poetry, p. 23.

8 Ibid. p. 25.

9 Ibid, p. 26.

10 "The Perfect Critic," p. 11.

11 Ibid. p. 5.

12 "The Function of Criticism," in Selected Essays, p. 19.

13 The Random House Dictionary of the English Language, 1970 ed.

14 "Imperfect Critics," p. 43.

15 "The Function of Criticism," p. 12.

16 "The Perfect Critic," p. 7.

17 "The Function of Criticism," p. 18.

18 "To Criticize the Critic," in To Criticize the Critic (New York: Farrar, Straus & Giroux, 1965), p. 13.

19 "Baudelaire," in Selected Essays, p. 371.

20 "To Criticize the Critic," p. 13.

21 "Goethe as the Sage," in On Poetry and Poets, p. 246.

22 Ibid. p. 247.

23 "The Perfect Critic," p. 12.

24 "Goethe as the Sage," p. 246.

25 Ibid. p. 249.

26 Ibid.

27 Ibid. p. 250.

28 "Religion and Literature," in Selected Prose, p. 97.

29 Freed, p. 167.

30 "Wordsworth and Coleridge," in The Use of Poetry, p. 80.

31 Ibid.

32 "The Uses of Great Men," in Works of Ralph Waldo Emerson (Boston: Houghton, Mifflin and Company, 1882), II, p. 20.

33 Brombert, p. 13.

34 Emerson, p. 18.

35 "Worsworth and Coleridge," p. 75.

36 Emerson, p. 24.

37 Emerson, p. 137; p. 153.

38 Mark Van Doren, ed., The Portable Emerson (New York: The Viking press, 1974), p. 157.

39 "Imperfect Critics," p. 37.

40 Emerson, p. 26.

41 "To Criticize the Critic," p. 17.

42 "Matthew Arnold," in The Use of Poetry, p. 104.

Notes to Chapter Four

[1] Emerson, p. 31.

[2] "Wordsworth and Coleridge," p. 71.

[3] Introduction to The Use of Poetry, p. 26.

[4] "Johnson as Critic and Poet," in On Poetry and Poets, p. 213.

[5] "The Music of Poetry," in On Poetry and Poets, p. 23.

[6] Ibid. p. 21.

[7] "Wordsworth and Coleridge," p. 74.

[8] Emerson, p. 21.

[9] "Wordsworth and Coleridge," p. 71.

[10] Freed, p. 221.

[11] "To Criticize the Critic," p. 18.

[12] "Review: Israfel," Nation and Athenaeum, 21 May 1927, p. 219.

[13] "Matthew Arnold," p. 106.

[14] "From Poe to Valéry," in To Criticize the Critic, p. 29.

[15] "Review: The Romantic Generation: If It Existed," Athenaeum, 4655 (18 July 1919), pp. 616-17.

[16] "Imperfect Critics," p. 18.

[17] "Johnson as Critic and Poet," p. 218.

[18] "The Frontiers of Criticism," in On Poetry and Poets," p. 119.

[19] "Wordsworth and Coleridge," p. 79.

[20] Introduction to The Use of Poetry, p. 27.

[21] Ibid. p. 29.

[22] Cornwell, p. 7.

23 "The Frontiers of Criticism," p. 124.

24 Ibid. p. 128.

25 "The Metaphysical Poets," in Selected Essays, p. 249.

26 From "Henry James," in Selected Prose, p. 152.

27 Ibid.

28 Note to "Wordsworth and Coleridge," p. 84.

29 "Review: Beyle and Balzac," Athenaeum, 4648 (30 May 1919), p. 392.

30 Cornwell, p. 12.

31 Ibid.

32 Introduction to The Use of Poetry, pp. 26-27.

33 "Review: Beyle and Balzac," p. 392.

34 Biographia Literaria in Coleridge: Selected Poetry and Prose, ed. Elisabeth Schneider (New York: Holt, Rinehart and Winston, 1962), p. 313.

35 "Tradition and the Individual Talent," in The Sacred Wood, p. 59.

36 Ibid. p. 58.

37 Kristian Smidt, Poetry and Belief in the Work of T.S. Eliot (London: Routledge and Kegan Paul, 1961; rpt. 1967), p. 40.

Notes to Chapter Five

1 "The Frontiers of Criticism," in On Poetry and Poets, p. 117.

2 "The Music of Poetry," in Selected Prose, p. 18.

3 "Imperfect Critics," in The Sacred Wood, p. 24.

4 "The Function of Criticism," in Selected Essays, p. 13.

5 Lucy, p. 51.

6 "Imperfect Critics," pp. 37-38.

7 "To Criticize the Critic," p. 22.

8 The Waste Land and Other Poems (New York: Harcourt Brace Jovanovich, 1975), pp. 27-54. All quotations are from this edition.

9 Erich Auerbach, "Figura," in Scenes from the Drama of European Literature (New York: Meridian World Publishing Company, 1959), p. 73.

10 "Tradition and the Individual Talent," in The Sacred Wood, p. 52.

11 Les Fleurs du mal (Paris: Editions Garnier Frères, 1961), p. 13

12 "Tradition and the Individual Talent," p. 52.

Notes to Chapter Six

1 See Coleridge: Selected Poetry and Prose. All quotations are from the edition.

2 Les Fleurs du mal (Paris: Editions Garnier Freres, 1961), pp. 35-36.

3 A.D. Moody, ed., The Waste Land in Different Voices (London: Edward Arnold, 1974), p. 58.

4 "Tradition and the Individual Talent," p. 50.

A SELECTED BIBLIOGRAPHY

Austin, Allen. T.S. Eliot: The Literary and Social Criticism. Bloomington: Indiana University Press, 1971.

Babbitt, Irving. The Masters of Modern French Criticism. New York: The Noonday Press, 1963.

_____, Rousseau and Romanticism. New York: Houghton Mifflin Company, 1919.

Bornstein, George. Transformations of Romanticism in Yeats, Eliot and Stevens. Chicago: University of Chicago Press, 1976.

Bradley, F.H. Appearance and Reality. London: George Allen Unwin Ltd., 1897.

Brombert, Victor. "T.S. Eliot and the Romantic Heresy." Yale French Studies, No.13 (1965), pp. 3-16.

Canary, Robert H. T.S. Eliot: The Poet and his Critics. Chicago: American Library Association, 1982.

Cornwell, Ethel F. The "Still Point". New Brunswick: Rutgers University Press, 1962.

Drew, Elizabeth. T.S. Eliot: The Design of His Poetry. New York: Charles Scribner's Sons, 1949.

Eliot, T.S. After Strange Gods. London: Faber and Faber Ltd., 1934.

_____, "The Development of Leibniz's Monadism." Monist, 26, No. 4 (Oct. 1916), pp. 534-56.

_____, "Leibniz's Monads and Bradley's Finite Centres." Monist, 26, No. 4 (Oct. 1916), pp. 566-76.

_____, On Poetry and Poets. New York: The Noonday Press, 1970.

_____, Selected Essays. New York: Harcourt, Brace and World, Inc., 1960.

_____, The Sacred Wood. London: Methuen & Company Ltd., 1964

_____, To Criticize the Critic. New York: Farrar Straus & Giroux, 1965.

_____, The Use of Poetry and the Use of Criticism. London: Faber and Faber Ltd., 1968.

Everett, Barbara. "Eliot's Marianne: 'The Waste Land' and Its Poetry of Europe." Review of English Studies, No. 31 (1980), pp. 41-53.

Freed, Lewis. T.S. Eliot: Aesthetics and History. LaSalle, Il.: Open Court Publishing Company, 1962.

Frye, Northrop. T.S. Eliot: An Introduction. Chicago: University of Chicago Press, 1963; Phoenix ed., 1981.

Gallup, Donald C. T.S. Eliot: A Bibliography. New York: Harcourt, Brace and World, 1969.

Hay, Eloise Knapp. T.S. Eliot's Negative Way. Cambridge, Ma.: Harvard University Press, 1982.

Kenner, Hugh. The Invisible Poet: T.S. Eliot. New York: Harcourt, Brace and World, 1959.

Kermode, Frank. Romantic Image. London: Routledge and Kegan Paul, 1957.

_____, ed. Selected Prose of T.S. Eliot. New York: Harcourt Brace Jovanovich and Farrar, Straus and Giroux, 1975.

Kirk, Russell. Eliot and His Age. New York: Random House, 1971.

Leavis, F.R. New Bearings in English Poetry. Ann Arbor: University of Michigan Press, 1960.

Lobb, Edward. T.S. Eliot and the Romantic Critical Tradition. London: Routledge and Kegan Paul, 1981.

Lucy, Sean. T.S. Eliot and the Idea of Tradition. New York: Barnes and Noble, Inc., 1960.

Margolis, John D. T.S. Eliot's Intellectual Development 1922-1939. Chicago: University of Chicago Press, 1972.

Matthiessen, F.O. The Achievement of T.S. Eliot. New York: Oxford University Press, 1958.

Moody, A.D., ed. The Waste Land in Different Voices. London: Edward Arnold, 1974.

_____, Thomas Stearns Eliot, Poet. Cambridge: Cambridge University Press, 1979.

Mowbray, Allan. T.S. Eliot's Impersonal Theory of Poetry. Lewisburg: Bucknell University Press, 1974.

Musgrove, S. T.S. Eliot and Walt Whitman. Wellington: New Zealand University Press, 1962.

Newton-De Molina, David, ed. The Literary Criticism of T.S. Eliot. London: The Athlone Press, University of London, 1977.

Nuttall, A.D. A Common Sky: Philosophy and the Literary Imagination. Berkeley: University of California Press, 1974.

Smidt, Kristian. Poetry and Belief in the Work of T.S. Eliot. London: Routledge and Kegan Paul, 1967.

Smith, Grover. T.S. Eliot's Poetry and Plays. Chicago: University of Chicago Press, 1950.

Spender, Stephen. T.S. Eliot. New York: The Viking Press, 1975.

Stead, C.K. The New Poetic. New York: Harper and Row, 1966.

Weinberg, Kerry. T.S. Eliot and Charles Baudelaire. The Hague: Mouton, 1969.

For Product Safety Concerns and Information please contact our EU representative GPSR@taylorandfrancis.com
Taylor & Francis Verlag GmbH, Kaufingerstraße 24, 80331 München, Germany

www.ingramcontent.com/pod-product-compliance
Lightning Source LLC
Chambersburg PA
CBHW070724020526

44116CB00031B/1811